Everyday Herbs in Spiritual Life

OTHER BOOKS AVAILABLE IN
THE ART OF SPIRITUAL LIVING SERIES

Everyday Herbs in Spiritual Life

A GUIDE TO MANY PRACTICES

Written and Illustrated by

MICHAEL J. CADUTO

Foreword by

ROSEMARY GLADSTAR

Walking Together, Finding the Way®
SKYLIGHT PATHS®
PUBLISHING
Woodstock, Vermont

Everyday Herbs in Spiritual Life:
A Guide to Many Practices

2007 First Printing
Text and Illustrations © 2007 by Michael J. Caduto

Library of Congress Cataloging-in-Publication Data
Caduto, Michael J.
Everyday herbs in spiritual life : a guide to many practices / written and illustrated by Michael J. Caduto ; foreword by Rosemary Gladstar.
p. cm.
Includes index.
ISBN-13: 978-1-59473-174-7 (pbk.)
ISBN-10: 1-59473-174-8 (pbk.)
1. Herbs—Religious aspects. I. Title.
BL444.C33 2007
203'.7—dc22

2007013651

10 9 8 7 6 5 4 3 2 1

Manufactured in the United States of America
Cover Design: Jenny Buono
Cover Art (from left to right): Mint © 2007 JupiterImages Corporation;
Borage © iStockphoto.com/emilyc; Calendula © iStockphoto.com/alle;
Lavender © iStockphoto.com/felinda; Bergamot © 2007 JupiterImages Corporation.

SkyLight Paths Publishing is creating a place where people of different spiritual traditions come together for challenge and inspiration, a place where we can help each other understand the mystery that lies at the heart of our existence.

SkyLight Paths sees both believers and seekers as a community that increasingly transcends traditional boundaries of religion and denomination—people wanting to learn from each other, *walking together, finding the way.*

SkyLight Paths, "Walking Together, Finding the Way," and colophon are trademarks of LongHill Partners, Inc., registered in the U.S. Patent and Trademark Office.

Walking Together, Finding the Way®
Published by SkyLight Paths Publishing
A Division of LongHill Partners, Inc.
Sunset Farm Offices, Route 4, P.O. Box 237
Woodstock, VT 05091
Tel: (802) 457-4000   Fax: (802) 457-4004
www.skylightpaths.com

For the
Green Hearts
and Healers
who nourish us all.

CONTENTS

LISTS OF HERBS

FOREWORD

I have been a long-time admirer of Michael Caduto's writings. He is a fellow Vermonter, a superb storyteller, and he writes of things dear to my heart. In *Everyday Herbs in Spiritual Life,* Michael offers a special gift to all of us who love plants and yearn for a deeper connection with the world around us. It is both a practical and spiritual guide to the use of herbs and how they can influence and affect our lives in the most positive ways.

There are endless books about herbs these days. The subject has become quite popular. There are books on herb gardening, herbal healing, on the culinary wonders of herbs, on traditional uses and folklore, and on clinical and scientific research. The mind and senses can wander almost endlessly through this wonderful maze of written information about these humble but very powerful plants. But there are few books that explore our deeper spiritual relationship to plants and fewer books that do so in such a practical and easily accessible manner.

That is what makes this book stand out among the plethora of herb books on my shelf and why I appreciate the author and his writings so much. This is a book that enters into the spiritual nature of our life on earth and how we as a species have developed in relationship to plants. Caduto has perfected the skill of weaving wisdom through the medium of stories. He takes us on a journey around the globe, collecting tales and traditions of herbal practices that people have used to help connect them to Spirit, or God in all of God's many radiant forms, and to the earth as well. We visit the spiritual traditions and herbal practices of Islam and Judaism, Hinduism and Buddhism, Christianity and indigenous First Nations people, among others. We learn how these cultures used plants in their everyday practices to enhance or deepen their connection to the spirit worlds or the world of spirit/God/Goddess. The stories, poems, and remembrances included herein are woven together into a beautiful tapestry of green wisdom that throughout history has anchored humankind to the earth and lifted us to the heavens.

Even more than just a book of history and folklore, Caduto instructs us with gentle guidance and simple steps on how to reclaim these traditions in our own lives. Throughout the book are many activities and projects that involve us with the green world and that are designed to bring more value into our lives. These activities are not only meaningful, but delightfully fun as well. They can be done with children, with elders, with neighbors and the neighborhood to bring deeper meaning and awareness to family events and celebrations. There are herbal activities to enhance meals, holidays, weddings, and births, and for grief and renewal—simple ceremonies that bring more life and significance to these events.

There is an ancient power and beauty embedded in plants and our relationship to them that serves to connect us both to our roots (our physical body) and to our spirit (our soul or spiritual self). Perhaps it is because plants themselves are so deeply rooted in the earth and reach upward to the heavens. Perhaps it is because they are so ancient, arriving on this earth long before we arrived as a species. Our life has evolved in relationship to our botanical friends. We depend on them for our very breath (they create and breathe out the oxygen we need to survive), our food, our medicine, and, yes, even for their spiritual guidance.

The teachings here in this wonderful book are designed to enter your heart and enrich your life. They are simple but profound; easy and accessible, rooted in history, passed down through the ages, designed to become part of your traditions, celebrations, and ceremonies. Plants sing to us in our gardens, reach out to us in the woodlands. They become part of us as food, spices, tea—and fill our lives with beauty. What would a world without plants be? They serve as medicine and manna not only for the body but spirit as well. *Everyday Herbs in Spiritual Life* is a feast for the spirit and will serve in the most beautiful way to bring herbs back into the sacred practice of everyday living.

Rosemary Gladstar, cofounder,
Sage Mountain Herbal Retreat Center
and Botanical Sanctuary

ACKNOWLEDGMENTS

Everyday Herbs in Spiritual Life was a joy to write. Ever since I worked on a small farm as a teenager, and later took my first undergraduate courses in agriculture and field botany, I have been passionate about plants. I love nothing more than to lead a group through an herb garden, or along a trail through the woodlands and meadows to interpret the facts, folklore, and fascinating lives of herbs all around us.

Within the pages of this book, I tried to convey the sense of a field experience. Fortunately, the writing took place while the snow blew past my window and plants slumbered, or I would never have been able to pull my wife, Marie Levesque Caduto, out of our garden long enough for her to sit down and read the manuscript. Marie offered many comments and suggestions and helped make certain that the activities work the way they should.

Holistic and eclectic, this book required expert readers from diverse backgrounds and interests. John Forti, Curator of Historic Landscapes at Strawbery Banke in Portsmouth, New Hampshire, gave generously of his time in the midst of a hectic schedule, reviewing the manuscript for accuracy and clarity. Many scholars offered their expertise about information concerning the various spiritual traditions, including Rabbi Mike Comins, Sanjeev Joshi, Girish Shirhatti, Mu Soeng, Sohaib N. Sultan, and Mark Ogilbee.

Maura D. Shaw, Ana Hernández, and Susan F. Jones all helped to shape the original concept of *Everyday Herbs*. In addition, Maura generously offered suggestions for activities, including one of my favorites, "Herbal Newlywed Blessings." Rosemary Gladstar—author, renowned herbalist, and founder of the Sage Mountain Herbal Retreat Center—kindly agreed to write the thoughtful foreword.

The neat, attractive volume you now hold was crafted by the wonderfully talented and patient staff of SkyLight Paths Publishing, who carry forth the good work of publisher Stuart M. Matlins. Every writer's spurts of creative growth need to be pruned, and both the editorial and design teams of SkyLight Paths are among the best gardeners of books. Project editors Mark Ogilbee; Lauren Seidman; and Sarah McBride; as well as Emily Wichland, vice president of editorial and production; gently weeded and shaped the manuscript into a book. Jenny Buono, Tim Holtz, and Kristi Menter, book and cover designers, crafted an elegant and accessible layout that artfully weaves together the many elements herein.

My deepest gratitude to the many friends and colleagues who have shared indigenous plant wisdom with me through the years. I hope this book honors the old ways, speaks well to others, and helps to keep the herbal traditions alive and growing.

INTRODUCTION

There is no creation
that does not have a radiance,
be it greenness or seed,
blossom or beauty.

It could not be creation
without it.
—Hildegard of Bingen, twelfth century

The history of humankind is recorded in flowers and leaves—in roots, seeds, and shoots. With tools of wood and ropes of bark, we harvested and crafted our way through the ages, relying on the bounty of our green providers for survival, health, and spiritual enrichment. Over time, we formed intimate bonds with certain plants that are no less connected or profound than our relationships with the world of flesh and bone. We draw our very breath from plants and glean from them the essence of life. Healing balms and savory spices strengthen our bodies and feed our souls.

Early Christian mystics, such as Hildegard of Bingen and Meister Eckhart, illuminate our common bond with nature. Hildegard

(1098–1179) was an author, artist, composer, and founder of a Benedictine convent in the German Rhineland that had strong Celtic roots. Both she and Meister Eckhart (1260–1328), who was born in the village of Erfurt in Thuringia (in modern-day Germany), were renowned mystics during a period of significant spiritual awakening within the Christian Church.

> Consider the divine spirit in the human soul.
> This spirit is not easily satisfied.
> It storms the firmament and scales the heavens
> trying to reach the spirit that drives the heavens.
> Because of this energy,
> everything in the world grows green,
> flourishes,
> and bursts into leaf.
>
> —*Meister Eckhart, thirteenth century*

Indigenous creation stories often tell of how people are made from plants. In the creation story of the Lacondon Maya from southern Mexico and northern Guatemala, the Creator and the Maker fashion the first people from cornmeal. Abenaki tradition in northeastern North America holds that the first people were made from stone, but they had cold, uncaring hearts. When these beings began to destroy Earth, the Creator took back the breath of life and turned them into mountains. Then a new people were carved from an ash tree; they stepped alive from its wood with hearts growing and green. To this day, special plants are used by the Abenaki to connect with the Creator. Those first people remembered always to give thanks for the gifts of creation, using tobacco—a powerful herb—as an incense offering. Sage, the herb of wisdom and virtue, is burned and used to cleanse a place, to purify an individual, or to bless a gathering of people.

Herbs are surrounded by mystery, and they possess the power to heal both body and spirit. The roots of the word *herb*, however, are mundane, coming from the Middle English *herbe* and the Latin *herba*, meaning "vegetation." But there is nothing commonplace about the role herbs play in spiritual ceremonies and celebrations in many faiths. A bitter herb called *maror* is eaten during the Jewish Seder meal that is shared on the eve of Passover. Its bitter taste, which evokes the hardships endured during the Israelites' time of slavery in Egypt, also elicits compassion among those who witness the pain of others. As with all dualities, the experience of suffering and mercy forms a circle.

In the Judaic tradition, Proverbs (15:17) tells of how caring and compassion trump wealth when the latter is accompanied by ill will:

> Better a dish of herbs
> when love is there,
> than a fattened ox
> and hatred to go with it.

In one moving passage from the Song of Songs (4:12–14), Israel is symbolized by a woman and a garden, whose virtues are extolled in the power of herbs:

> She is a garden enclosed,
> my sister, my promised bride;
> a garden enclosed,
> a sealed fountain.
> Your shoots form an orchard
> of pomegranate trees,
> the rarest of essences are yours:
> spikenard and saffron,
> calamus and cinnamon,
> with all incense-bearing trees;
> myrrh and aloes,
> with the subtlest odors.

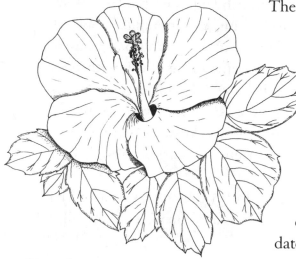

Hibiscus flowers are used to create a traditional Ramadan beverage.

The prophecies of the Qur'an emphasize the healing aspects of herbs. *Al-Tibb al-Nabawi* (*Medicine of the Prophet*) includes many practices that entail the use of Qur'anic verse, indigenous herbs, water, oil, and ornaments in traditional Islamic healing. During Ramadan, Muslim faithful partake of and use powerful herbs and foods—including dates, hibiscus flowers, and *miswak* (a tree twig)—whose use can be traced back to the prophet Muhammad. Rosewater is also used as a pleasant essence that lifts spirits and brings calm during the trial of the fast. Hibiscus is refreshing and is high in vitamin C, which fortifies the body's defenses against illness and helps maintain normal kidney function. Dates lead the body gently into a first meal after the daily fast. A frayed *miswak* twig serves to cleanse the mouth during and after the fast.

Christian tradition is steeped in the use of herbs for maintaining and healing body and soul. In the twelfth century, Hildegard of Bingen wrote *Physica, Liber Simplicis Medicinae (Medicine or Book of Simple Medicine),* a groundbreaking book on health and healing that explains the properties and uses for healing herbs. In Hildegard's vision of cosmic wholeness, to be green and moist is to be spiritually vital and alive. Health is built upon virtue and is rooted in a state of living in balance, receptive to sharing the lives of those around us. In one of her paintings that depicts the renewal of heaven and earth, Hildegard shows the elements of the cosmos to be water, herbs, flowers, stars, and the sky.

This book introduces the reader to the power of herbs to enhance and enrich our spiritual journeys. Touchstones along the path include discussions of historical and contemporary uses of herbs; readings of wisdom from many spiritual books; and herbal traditions from a wide range of religious and spiritual paths, including Jewish, Christian, Islamic, Buddhist, Hindu, and Native American and other indigenous teachings. These inspiring explorations are complemented by a wealth of activities, including:

- Making candles infused with herbs that promote balance and centering
- Drying herbs and herb flowers to create art that is inspired by faith
- Crafting herbal wreaths, pillows, soaps, and other creations from herbs chosen for their spiritual qualities
- Preparing herbal teas, infused oils, meals, and condiments chosen for their ability to nurture, strengthen, and heal
- Making herbal potpourri and sachets that nourish the soul
- Making and using incense and smudge sticks to imbue clarity and purity
- Fashioning herbal crafts as a way of having fun and relaxing through creative expression
- Designing a simple herb garden of plants that symbolize spiritual wholeness and balance
- Creating spaces in which to use herbs for reflection and meditation

Everyday Herbs in Spiritual Life is organized by major themes—familiar reference points that are springboards for activities and spiritual reflections from different faiths. Each chapter focuses on specific practices for using and experiencing herbs in your spiritual life.

Chapter 1 explores the healing qualities of herbs for all aspects of body, mind, and spirit, including cultivated herbals and wild medicinals. Activities use herbs for spiritual balance and wholeness, aromatherapy, indigenous healing practices, purification, protection, and solace.

Chapter 2 looks at beauty and the relationship between aesthetics and virtue among many spiritual traditions and in our inner lives. Activities show how our lives can be enriched through sensory experiences with herbs.

Chapter 3 provides meals, rituals, and ceremonies centered on the use of herbs for feeding the body and spirit and for growing an interfaith community. Activities include holiday crafts and celebrations, as well as herbal practices for giving thanks.

Chapter 4 looks into the heart of the Circle of Life. It shows how to use herbs as a means of promoting balance and for connecting with all of creation: life and death, grief and renewal, memorials, love and attraction, making connections, weddings, marital blessings, births, and babies.

Chapter 5 is a journey through sacred herb gardens that reflect visions and meanings of the cosmos and of paradise from many spiritual traditions, including Judaic scripture; Buddhist mandalas; Hindu sacred gardens; Christian monastic gardens; Islamic gardens; Arab gardens; sacred Egyptian herbs; indigenous Abenaki traditions; Celtic and Druid lore; and Greek and Roman myth, magic, and labyrinths.

Chapter 6 focuses on the reflective and centering uses of herbs for meditation, inner journeys, and artistic expression.

Chapter 7 provides practical tips for choosing and obtaining herbs, for designing and growing an herb garden, for growing herbs indoors, and for harvesting and preserving herbs.

Herbs are a joy and a blessing. Walk the pathways of these pages and experience the fun and mystery of herbs. Allow herbs to teach you and to reveal their beauty and sensory delights. Share in the creative power of herbs. Invite herbs into the rhythms of your spiritual life, and allow them to enrich and heal your inner being. Truly, herbs are a gift from the Creator.

HERBS BY ANY OTHER NAME

Before diving into this holistic experience of herbs, an important question needs to be addressed: what is an herb? By some definitions, herbs are plants that are not woody. They are also defined as any aromatic plant that is used for seasoning and medicine. In this book, I define *herb* broadly to include plants that are commonly regarded as herbs, such as basil and cardamom, as well as other plants whose parts are commonly used for food, medicine, and spiritual practices, such as frankincense and myrrh (gum resins), cinnamon and willow (tree barks), ginger and mandrake (roots), and saffron (dried stigmas of crocus flowers).

A WORD ABOUT SAFETY

Many herbs are powerful natural medicines and should only be used under the expert care and direction of a medical doctor. Herbs should not be used alone to treat serious illnesses. Consult with your physician before introducing herbs into your health regimen.

Herbs for
Healing

Acacia
Agrimony (M)
Aloe (M)
Anise (M, I)
Balsam (N)
Basil (M, I)
Basswood (N)
Bay, sweet (M, I)
Bergamot (bee
  balm) (N)
Betony (M)
Birch, yellow (N)
Black cumin (I)
Bougainvillea (N)
Calendula (M)
Camphor (M, I)
Caraway (M, I)
Cardamom (I)
Catnip (catmint) (M)
Cedar, white
  (arbor vitae) (N)
Celery (M)
Chamomile (M, I)
Chervil (M)
Chicory (M, I)
Chives (M)
Cinnamon (M, I)
Citron (I)
Clove (M)
Coriander (M, I)
Cumin (M, I)

Dill (M, I)
Elm, slippery (N)
Eucalyptus
Fennel (M, I)
Frankincense (I)
Galanga (M)
Garlic (M, I)
Ginger (M)
Ginseng (N)
Hibiscus (I)
Hops (N)
Horehound (M)
Horseradish (M)
Hyacinth (I)
Hyssop (M)
Jasmine (I)
Jewelweed (N)
Lavender (M, I)
Licorice (M)
Lily (M, I)
Lovage (M)
Maple, striped (N)
Marjoram (M, I)
Milkweed (N)
Mint (M, I)
Mustard (M, I)
Myrrh (M)
Myrtle (M, I)
Narcissus (M, I)
Nutmeg (M)
Orange (M)

Oregano (I)
Parsley (M, I)
Patchouli
Pennyroyal (M, N)
Pepper (M)
Peppermint (M, I)
Periwinkle (M, I)
Polypody, fern (M)
Rose (M, I)
Rosemary (M)
Rue (M, I)
Saffron (M, I)
Sage (M)
Sandalwood (I)
Savory (M, I)
Sorrel (M, I)
Sumac (red
  berries) (N)
Sweetfern (N)
Tansy (M)
Thyme (M)
Tobacco (N)
Verbena
Violet (M, I, N)
Wild marjoram (M)
Wild thyme (M, I)
Willow (I, N)
Wormwood (M, I)
Yarrow (M, N)

(M) = Medieval monastic gardens   (I) = Islamic gardens   (N) = Native American herbals

1

HEALING HERBALS

Although the northeast wind may hinder the fruit,
it marvelously preserves the spirits,
and health will ensure pleasure for those
who seek that in the garden,
and not fruit.

—Piero de'Crescenzi,
Liber Ruralium Commodorum
(Book of Rural Arts), 1304–1309

I crush the delicate, fern-like leaves of yarrow between my fingers and inhale a scent that speaks of healing power. This is not the medicine that comes in a bottle, but something deeper that emanates from the Source. Before the tube of ointment came the organic root that draws its healing essence from the soil. Beyond capsules and pills lie unguents and elixirs distilled from seed and leaf, extracted from root and flower.

Physical healing is the stepsister of total wellness. In Islamic traditional medicine, *health* is attained when a person reaches a state of balance among the four elements, or *humors*: air, water, earth, and fire. The eleventh-century herbalist Ibn Sina wrote of the primary functions of the heart (seat of emotion), the liver (nourishment), and the brain (motion and feeling). The Spirit energizes and enlivens these vital organs. Because blood flows to our heart from our brain, human beings have a palpable sense that feelings arise from, and dwell within, our hearts. Oil pressed from the needles of cedar invigorates both our physical and our spiritual well-being; it promotes balance, heightens our sense of spiritual connection, and strengthens our immune system.

ROOTS OF HEALING AND MEDICINE

Herbs have been essential to spiritual beliefs and practices throughout time and history. In ancient Egypt, Ramses III used cumin as a sacred offering to the sun god Ra at Heliopolis. Tutankhamen's tomb was adorned with a pharaonic floral collar woven of chamomile flowers, whose minute yellow petals reflected the light that penetrated the tomb when it was first opened after being shrouded in darkness for more than 3,300 years.

A millennium after Tutankhamen's reign, there lived a renowned healer and botanist named Artemesia, who was both sister and wife to King Mausolus of Greece and Persia. Her namesake is now borne by the powerful herb called wormwood, *Artemesia absinthium*. Yarrow's genus, *Achillea*, traces its roots to the Battle of Troy in Homer's saga the *Iliad*, where Achilles used this potent herb to stem the blood flow from the wounds of his men.

Herbalism has long been steeped in myth and lore, but the origins of Western medicine lie in quiet alcoves and along worn stone paths of lovingly tended gardens of ancient temples, mosques, and monasteries. Here, each herb was nurtured and its healing properties meticulously recorded. The oldest extant book of herbs was written and illustrated on parchment in 300 BCE by Diocles of Carystos. Another ancient treatise consists of five volumes dating from 50 to 68 CE and is named for its author, Pedanios Dioscorides. This work, which is also known as the *Juliana Anicia Codex*, is the first known compendium of medicine and medicinal plants. The *Dioscorides* describes the medical uses, properties, and methods of preparing six hundred different species.

Among the early medicinals were those inspired by Islamic royal gardens, where native plants and exotics were cultivated. Abu Hanifaal-Dinawari created one of the first Islamic herbals, the *Kitab al-Nabat (A Work on Plants)*, in the ninth century. Two hundred years later, in the Iranian village of Ghaznavid, a historian and scientist named al-Bayruni created the *Kitab al-Saydanah fi al-Tibb (Book on Pharmacy)*, a compendium of plants from

> *God has anointed you*
> *with the oil of gladness....*
> *myrrh and aloes*
> *waft from your robes.*
>
> —Psalms 45:8

around the world. The twelfth-century botanist al-Sharif al-Idrisi described the medicinal plants of Spain and North Africa in his book *al-Jami al-Nabat,* or *Book of Plants*. These are just a few of the notable scholarly works from a long line of early Islamic botanists.

The first Arabic translation of *Dioscorides* appeared in Baghdad in the ninth century. At about this time, medicine and medicinal plants also began to proliferate in the medieval gardens of Christian monasteries. Monks and cloister gardens became an important source of medicine during the Middle Ages. In time, medical schools in Salerno, Montpellier, and other locations built on this monastic tradition and offered formal training in medicine.

One early manuscript that has survived since 1525 is titled *Herbys Necessary for a Gardyn* and is now known as *The Fromond List*. The author suggests that the scent of certain plants, including bay leaves, fennel, violet, mint, and rose, will help prevent illnesses from entering a house. One of the great quests of Western medicine—the cure for colds— seems to have its roots in medieval monastic gardens. A remedy from this time recommends combining these herbs to cure a cold: lovage, wild thyme, catmint, parsley, celery, fennel, and pennyroyal. An alternative remedy consists of an amalgam of herbal and mineral powders, including cinnamon, aloe, clove, camphor, nutmeg, ginger, galanga, pearl, and ivory. In other words, everything but the cloister's kitchen sink.

The root of the word *medicine* lies in the Latin *medicus*, "physician," and *medēri*, "to heal." Herbs possess a multitude of healing attributes that are still being discovered. To simply imbibe the pleasant and varied scents of herbs makes us feel more alive and healthy. Fragrance itself is one of the great healers and has inspired the practice of aromatherapy. Massaging with particular essential oils can help relax or stimulate the mind and spirit, cleanse and heal the skin, improve circulation, and alleviate stress.

Well-chosen oils and fragrances can allay our anxieties and instill a sense of calm. Oil of frankincense helps strengthen and renew our faith and bring life into balance. Essential oil of clove protects and inspires courage. Patchouli invigorates and raises our spirits. Romans saw wisdom and glory embodied in oil from leaves of bay, a tree that was connected to prophetic incantations from the oracles in Greek mythology—those who presided over the Delphi Temple of Apollo. To this day, bay leaf garlands adorn the architectural details of grand buildings and a *laureate* is honored with a crown of laurels woven of twigs plucked from branches of the sweet bay, *Laurus nobilis*.

> You who pay the tithe
>   of mint and dill and cumin ...
> have neglected the weightier matters
>   of the law—
> justice, mercy, and good faith.
>
> —Matthew 23:23

If creation consists of the myriad manifestations of the One, then all beings are truly interconnected and true health for any individual can only exist when considering the well-being of the whole. Hildegard of Bingen taught that living justly and openly with others is an essential aspect of health. This creates a circle of relationships that exist in a dynamic balance. A virtuous life is a healthy life. Coriander speaks to this way of being, with its attributes of modesty, of value quietly held. Simple catnip attracts love, health, and happiness.

Hildegard of Bingen, as she is now known, was born in 1098, the tenth child of a wealthy family. When she was eight years old,

Hildegard was sent to live in a small religious community of women who were associated with the Benedictine monastery of Mount Saint Disibode. There she entered into tutelage under an eldress named Jutta. Thirty years later, when Jutta died, Hildegard was chosen to serve as abbess. When the women's community at Mount Saint Disibode grew too large for their quarters, they departed with Hildegard,

> *It is I, God,*
> *who give you healing.*
>
> —Exodus 16:26

who went on to establish her own Benedictine community of women near Bingen.

In Hildegard's day, women were not allowed to publicly express their religious thoughts and inspirations in writing. It was only after the Archbishop of Mainz declared her writings to be inspired by God that Hildegard was granted permission to write. The books and music that she created before she died at the age of eighty-two inspired a spiritual movement that has proven timeless.

Throughout her long and productive life, Hildegard was guided by Benedict's Rule, which taught that healing others who are ill is the central purpose in life. True healing did not originate with the healer, but was divinely inspired.

MEDICINE KEEPERS, HERBAL HEALERS

The paradigm of healing as inclusive of both us and other, of body and spirit, came home to me in an unexpected way more than twenty years ago. Through a mutual love and respect for Earth, I met many indigenous peoples from the Northeast. Most of these friends and colleagues are of Abenaki, Mohawk, Narragansett, and Wampanoag ancestry.

Medicine ceremonies, such as the sweat lodge, are sacred to native peoples. For this reason, they are meant to be conducted only by members of indigenous cultures who are recognized and experienced healers. Here in the Northeast, the traditional dome-shaped lodge is fashioned from saplings of the healing willow tree, then covered in skins, using a flap for a door. No one enters without first being cleansed in spirit with smoke from a smudge stick of dried sage.

As we entered the sweat lodge, we moved sunwise around the circle until settling in our places. In the center a small firepit glowed red. Sprigs of needles from the white cedar curled up and leapt into flame as they were crumbled into the heat. As a ladle of springwater was poured onto the hot rocks, steam and heat penetrated deep into our lungs. The prayers began.

Indigenous medicine heals body and spirit. Among the Abenaki, a person's medicine resides in both the physical being and the life force. Vital and alive, the life force embodies emotion, energy, and health. The wellness of a person's spirit depends on the state of his or her mind and the strength of relationships with Earth and Sky. To live in balance is to keep one's medicine strong, to share a kind heart guided by a clear mind.

Medicine, *nebizon*, is sacred to the Abenakis—the source of one's strength, wisdom, and power in the cosmos. *Nebizon* encompasses all aspects of life that act on body, mind, and spirit, as well as one's attitude toward them. This includes all forms of knowledge, such as the advice of elders, natural and cultural laws, and lessons that arise from stories and oral tradition. *Nebizon* is sought through the vision quest, during ceremonies, by fasting, by the use of healing herbs, and by seeking both joy and satisfaction in life. Adults carry a medicine bag, *nebizoninoda*, in which they keep special stones, herbs, and other natural objects that represent their helpers in nature and bear testimony to the power received through their life experiences, particularly during the rite of passage and in later vision quests. Corn, tobacco, sage, bundles of healing herbs, tree barks, and sunflower seeds are often kept in the *nebizoninoda* for use when giving thanks and making offerings.

Knowledge of native herbalism is essential for anyone who desires to heal others. Apprenticing under an established healer is a discipline that takes several years. The student often learns how to treat a variety of diseases, illnesses, and injuries, and then specializes in certain related groups of diseases and the plants associated with treating them. Roots, barks, extracts, and oils are used to create poultices, teas, and salves. Knowledge of each specific plant—what it can be used to treat and how to prepare the healing parts of that plant—can only be acquired through lengthy and intensive training. Roots need to be boiled and softened to make a poultice for dressing wounds; teas have to be extracted to treat stomach upsets, colds, and sore throats. Persistent fevers are treated by purification in the sweat lodge followed by a plunge directly into cold water after emerging from the intense heat. General body aches are wrapped in heated strips of sod that are then enshrouded in mats woven from plant fibers.

This practice of utilizing the healing power of Earth has a kinship with the Celtic tradition that was practiced in the 1800s by Scottish coal miners in Fife. Whenever a miner inhaled toxic gas, he was brought to the surface. A hole was dug, a plug of turf was removed, and the miner stuck his head into the hole to inhale the cleansing vapors of the humus. That night the miner slept with his head upon the piece of turf as a pillow.

The tradition of herbal healing among indigenous peoples is woven into the fabric of their faith and daily lives in ways similar to those of the Israelites from earlier times. Smoke from sage smudge sticks is used to clear and purify both the human spirit and the dwelling places. Romans also considered sage to be a sacred plant, to be harvested only after cleansing the feet and donning ceremonial white tunics. A sacrifice of wine and bread was then offered before picking the sage. Aromatic stems were woven into wreaths.

From China to North America, the virtues of sage include good health, a good domestic life, and

Using a smudge stick for cleansing and purification.

longevity. Sage has long served to allay the universal human awareness of the impermanence of our existence. Rue is its herbal alter ego, whose name comes from the Old English *hrēowan*, "to distress" or "to make sad." Rue represents grief and sorrow, and yet is infused with the soothing comforts of mercy, sympathy, and forgiveness.

When Cortés and his Spanish soldiers invaded Tenochtitlán in 1519, they discovered vast gardens in which the Aztec (Nahua or Tenochca) civilization cultivated more than two thousand species of plants. At that time, the healing practices and herbal medicines of the Americas were far beyond the rudimentary healing arts practiced in Europe. *Tzapotlatena* is the Aztec goddess of pharmacy and *Tonantzin* the Earth goddess or goddess of medicine, particularly of herbal cures. Tonantzin's charge included stewardship for every living thing on Earth.

Our lives are over in a breath.
Our life lasts for seventy years,
eighty with good health,
but they all add up to anxiety and trouble—
over in a trice,
and then we are gone.

—Psalms 90:9–10

There are two kinds of Aztec healers: the *tepati*, or herbalists, and the *ticitl*, traditional vessels of indigenous wisdom. Other healers specialized in treating skin diseases as well as pediatric and gynecological illnesses. Various herbs are still used for healing, just as the Aztecs were using them nearly five hundred years ago: artemesia to treat intestinal parasites, acacia for dyspepsia and headache, bougainvillea for coughs, and eucalyptus for spiritual healing and purification.

Among the indigenous peoples who continue to ply their ancient healing ways are the *tinesmegelen*, the Tuareg medicine women who live in the lands of Mali and Niger in West Africa. This seminomadic indigenous culture practices medicine, *amagal*, by drawing from a deep well of indigenous traditions combined with Muslim beliefs. As with the tenets of some Christian, Native American, and Islamic traditions, the Tuareg believe that illness has its roots in a body that is out of balance or a spirit that is under duress. A state of health comes only to those who treat others well and have kind words for friends, neighbors, and family members.

Tuareg medicine takes the form of healing barks from more than one hundred different trees and shrubs, which are carried in a calabash *ten*, or medicine pot. Herbs are often cooked and steeped like a tea. Tuareg medicinal training takes a minimum of four years to master. It includes sound nutrition and herbal remedies to heal problems in the four major locuses where illnesses dwell: the stomach, liver, back, and blood. Those who possess the gift of healing massage, the *tamadas*, use touch to find and diagnose an illness. Their touch then conveys powerful thoughts, feelings, and healing energy. Healing sometimes involves touching the earth and then placing the other hand upon the afflicted place to draw the illness out of the patient and through the healer into the earth, or *amadal*.

In Tuareg oral tradition, the first healing barks came into the world in the hands of two babies born to a woman who was slain by her jealous husband. One young woman grew up to heal by touch and the other by deft application of the medicine barks. To this day, trees are a sacred symbol of life from which come the blessings, *al baraka*. Healing songs are used and illnesses are often treated

Do not place your trust in herbs or seek cures in human advice, for although we read that medicine was established by God, it is He who makes the sick whole.

—Cassiodorus, ca. 551 CE, *Institutiones Divinarum et Saecularium Litterarum (Institutes of Divine and Secular Literature)*

in the shadow of the tree that has given the gift of that particular healing bark.

Medicine women live where the earth is sacred, or *al hima*: places where the blessings dwell. Although it requires a lengthy apprenticeship to become a healer, to learn the rituals and how to prepare the healing barks, the Tuareg believe that the only true power to heal comes from God.

Theirs must be a strong faith, for Tuareg healers have discovered a cure for the common cold.

IN THE BALANCE

We who live in the Americas do not have to visit other continents to witness traditional herbal healing firsthand. Indigenous peoples are all around us; their knowledge and wisdom are there for those who have an open mind and eyes to see. Native healing is both practical and sacred: it helps the afflicted achieve a life synchronous with the dance of the cosmos. The Abenaki believe that Mother Earth, *Pegwiigawes,* gives the air and water to the People, the food and plants that heal. She has the power to restore balance between people and the natural world, between a man and a woman, among a person's body, mind, and spirit. A healer is a person of power—a man, *medawlinno,* or a woman, *medawlinnoska*—who stands at the heart of this relationship and can intercede to help others maintain and restore this balance. This often means finding a way to cure an unknown illness, or one that persists for a long time. Healing is often a legacy among the Abenaki; many healers are descended from a long, venerable lineage steeped in the traditions that are used to bring a state of health, *sôgelamalsowôgan,* to others in the community.

Indigenous healers must master an intimate knowledge of the life cycle of every medicinal plant. Many plants need to be used in season, such as sweetfern leaves and jewelweed sap to alleviate the itch of poison ivy, and milkweed sap for treating warts. With the coming of the Harvest Moon, *Temezôwas,* many of the medicinal plants are gathered and dried or otherwise prepared for later use, such as yellow birch bark for diarrhea and rheumatism, basswood bark and slippery elm bark for infected wounds, the bark of striped maple for creating a poultice to reduce swollen limbs, willow bark for a tea to treat colds and muscle aches, and the red berries of sumac for making a tea to sooth a sore throat.

Traditionally, when a desirable plant for food, medicine, or material is found, indigenous peoples of the Northeast weed around it to reduce competition for sunlight and soil nutrients from neighboring plants. During times of drought, they water certain patches of wild plants to help them survive, and even pick seeds as they mature and spread them around to enlarge the stand.

It is imperative to be especially careful and respectful when picking and gathering medicinal plants. Permission is asked of the plant and of the Creator, *Kici Niwaskw*. A small amount is taken and only from abundant patches of plants, merely thinning out the growth and leaving many of the plants behind to continue the next generation. Never is the tallest "Grandmother" plant picked from any growth of medicinal plants: she, who is the progenitor of all others in that place, is left behind out of respect and to assure the fecundity of her kind.

~

For reasons of personal safety as well as spiritual connection, take great care when using herbs of any kind for medicine or food. Some herbs can have toxic effects if used wrongly, when taken while pregnant, or if you suffer from allergies. Some of the most healthful herbs can have deleterious effects when ingested in too great a quantity. Even the Bible clearly warns us of the danger of using herbs without knowledge. When a soup was prepared using an unidentified wild edible—a bitter fruit— Elisha's men ate it and cried out, "Man of God, there is death in the pot!" (2 Kings 4:40–41).

A Touch of Scent

MATERIALS:

Small glass jar with secure cap

2 ounces massage base oil (almond or olive)

20–30 total drops essential herbal oils:
musk, clove, and camphor for a traditional Islamic scent
or others of your choice—rose, hyacinth, orange peel,
lavender, balsam, narcissus, white jasmine,
marjoram, saffron, lily, myrtle, chamomile,
hyssop, or bergamot

Use aromatherapy as medicine for the spirit. Among Eastern and Western traditions, medicine—our life force—is strongest when body, mind, and spirit exist in balance within the self, and in our relationship with all of creation.

Be certain to use *essential oils* that have been extracted from plants to include their myriad complex ingredients and compounds. Oils that contain only the fragrance or scent—some of which are now synthetically produced—do not possess the healing qualities of essential oils.

1. You can create massage oil as a form of medicine for the spirit. To a small glass jar, add 2 ounces of oil as a base. Olive oil has been used historically, or almond oil makes a good substitute because it keeps well and has little scent of its own.

2. Now add 20 to 30 drops of the essential herbal oil of your choice.

3. Gently massage the neck and temples with oil of balsam to ease a troubled mind. Rub oil of rose, lavender, mint, or thyme into the temples to reduce tension and quell a headache. Share a massage of bergamot oil with someone you love as a gift of happiness and contentment.

Growing an Herbal Heart

Materials:

Medium-sized pot
Sweet potting soil
Heart-shaped wire trellis (or wire coat hanger)
Rosemary seedling
Pruning clippers
Tea ball
1 ounce oil of rosemary
2 ounces water
1 ounce isopropyl alcohol

Alternative: Plant a lavender or marjoram seedling.

Rosemary is well known for its ability to strengthen the spiritual bond between those who are in love. It bolsters the memory and is a symbol of fidelity. This gentle herb, bearing flowers of pink or blue, protects from fever and is said to have safeguarded Mary, mother of Jesus, when she fled to Egypt.

1. You can grow your own heart from a healing plant. Prepare a medium-sized pot with sweet, fertile potting soil.
2. Obtain a heart-shaped wire trellis from a greenhouse. If you cannot find one, bend the hanger into the shape of a heart with the hooked end at the bottom.
3. Bury the hook and use it to anchor the heart well in the potted soil.
4. Plant a rosemary seedling at the base of the wire frame.
5. As the plant grows, train two main branches such that one branch climbs up each side of the heart.
6. There are many ways to use rosemary. Allow wandering shoots to grow, then trim them with clippers and weave them into wreaths and garlands. Prune and dry errant shoots, then burn these as incense to enjoy the pleasing aroma and for use as an

(continued on next page)

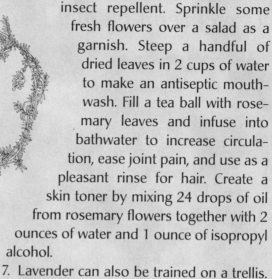

"Growing an Herbal Heart" with rosemary.

insect repellent. Sprinkle some fresh flowers over a salad as a garnish. Steep a handful of dried leaves in 2 cups of water to make an antiseptic mouthwash. Fill a tea ball with rosemary leaves and infuse into bathwater to increase circulation, ease joint pain, and use as a pleasant rinse for hair. Create a skin toner by mixing 24 drops of oil from rosemary flowers together with 2 ounces of water and 1 ounce of isopropyl alcohol.

7. Lavender can also be trained on a trellis. The name of this popular herb comes from the Latin *lavare*, "to wash." Its lovely, grayish-green leaves have been grown for centuries to provide the pleasant scent they impart to the home, fabrics, and bathwater. Oil from lavender flowers protects from illness, eases headaches and sore muscles, and provides gentle relief from the pain of mild burns and insect bites. Infused in bath oil, lavender imparts cleanliness and purity, reduces skin blemishes, alleviates anxiety, lifts the spirits, and encourages sweet love.

8. Marjoram, too, can be trained on the heart trellis. Aphrodite, the Greek goddess of love, brought this aromatic herb into the world as a symbol of happiness.

ALTERNATIVE: Plant rosemary, lavender, or marjoram in your garden, or in a pot, and prune it into the shape of a heart as it grows to create your own topiary.

Purification and Protection: Smudging

MATERIALS:

Sage smudge stick or 6 to 12 fine sage twigs that are
6 to 8 inches long

Cotton string or fine hemp twine

Scissors

Pruning clippers

Matches

Prayer or recitation of your choice

NOTE: Garden sage *(Salvia officinalis)* is commonly used, and is native to southern Europe. Several species of sage are native to the arid lands of western and southwestern North America, including white sage, *Salvia apiana.*

ALTERNATIVE: Substitute twigs of lavender when making the smudge stick.

It may seem ironic that the use of smoke for purification and protection is called smudging. To most people, smudging is the use of smoke to repel insects or protect an orchard from frost. In the Native American tradition, smudging is a spiritual practice that employs smoke to periodically clear a home or other space, to renew the positive spiritual energy. You may also want to clear a home after something has happened and left a negative feeling or presence, such as after you have received bad news, when a series of injuries occurs, after numbers of people have gathered for a raucous party, when an illness lingers, after someone has died, or after a bad fight. Smudge to cleanse and purify, to renew positive spiritual energy, and to heal.

Smudging can also help us to clear our own stale thoughts and actions in order to create an opening, to offer an invitation for new growth, for positive experiences and spiritual advancement.

1. Bundles of dried sage, called smudge sticks, can be obtained at most herb shops. Or you can make your own by taking 6 to 12

(continued on next page)

fine sage twigs, trimming them 6 to 8 inches long, and tying them tightly together into a bundle with cotton string. Be certain to make each wrapping of string around the bundle be a separate piece with its own knot, or else the smudge stick will come undone as it burns down.

2. Light the end of the bundle and allow it to burn briefly, as you would a stick of incense, then blow out the flame. I like to start outside the house and simply walk around, creating an unbroken ring of smoke. As you slowly circle, gently wave the smudge stick from side to side while softly saying a quiet prayer or simply making a personal request to expel any negative energy. Now enter the home and continue this process, entering each room where you sense a need to clear the energy and restore a positive spiritual balance.

3. Have a friend take the active smudge stick and use it to slowly trace a circle of smoke around your entire body. Hold your arms out and lift each foot in turn so that the smudge stick can completely encircle and pass beneath you. Now exchange roles and use the smudge stick to perform a clearing on your friend. Smudging with sage on a regular basis is a way to heal the effects of negative energy, maintain spiritual health, restore balance in the home, and enable a positive home life to flourish.

ALTERNATIVE: You can also use a lavender smudge stick. Tightly tie together a bundle of lavender stalks, 6 to 8 inches long, and use as directed above for a sage smudge stick. Lavender is used for purification, peace, and clarity of vision.

Purification and Protection: Scents of Protection

MATERIALS:

Potpourri

Candle

Wreath or incense made from one or more of the herbs listed in this activity

Matches

1. Use potpourri, scented candles, herbal wreaths, and incense to protect the spirit of your home. Choose from among these herbs and their virtues:

- Bay, for protection against disease and negative spirits
- Clove, for protection and courage
- Fennel, mint, rose, and violet, to ward off illness in the house
- Rosemary, burned as incense to cleanse air in a room where someone is ill

Purification and Protection: Garlic Wreath

MATERIALS:

2 dozen cloves garlic (per necklace)
Sturdy thread
Stout needle
Thimble
Scissors

1. String cloves of garlic onto sturdy thread using a stout needle and a thimble.
2. Hang a necklace over each doorway as powerful protection from negative spiritual energy.

ALTERNATIVE: Another option is to eat a meal that is heavily flavored with garlic before going to any crowded place. You will then have a proven ally in warding off any person who may pose a threat to faith and spirit, and everyone else!

Cards for Celebration

MATERIALS:

> *Dried and pressed flower petals and leaves of your choice:*
> *thyme, parsley, cinnamon, or catnip*
>
> *Blank cards*
>
> *Pencil*
>
> *Scissors*
>
> *White glue*
>
> *Cotton swab*
>
> *Pen*
>
> *Small elegant box*
>
> *Soft packing material (such as cotton)*

1. Use the dried flower petals and leaves of herbs to create small works of art on the fronts of blank cards to send for holidays, celebrations, and remembrances. Choose various colors and textures of herbs to create an image that will be meaningful to the recipient. Use herbs that convey the particular virtues, strengths, or qualities that you want to give to your friend or loved one, such as thyme for happiness and affection, parsley for festivity, cinnamon for love and good fortune, or catnip for health and happiness.

2. Sketch a pattern on the card in pencil. When you are satisfied with the design, use the cotton swab to outline the pattern with glue, spreading evenly.

3. Sprinkle the herbs onto the glue to create the desired pattern. Tap off excess herbs. To form layers, glue herbs on individually.

4. When the glue has dried, inscribe a personal note inside the card and include a brief description of the herbs and what they impart on the back of the card.

5. Place your card carefully in a small, elegant box and surround it with soft packing material.

Cards for Solace

MATERIALS:

Dried and pressed flower petals and leaves of your choice: calendula, lavender, patchouli, rose, rosemary, or rue

The rest of the materials listed in "Cards for Celebration," page 27.

1. Use the same techniques and materials described for "Cards for Celebration" to create an herbal card to express solace for someone's loss and to share sympathy with feelings of sorrow. Alternatively, address a card directly to someone you have personally lost in order to honor what that person means in your life. In this latter case, deliver the card to that person's resting place and offer a prayer.

2. Here are some herbs to use for a card of solace:

- Calendula for remembrance and a scent that soothes one who is suffering
- Lavender for healing and protection from harmful thoughts
- Patchouli as a calming influence and for lifting spirits
- Rose for forgiveness and as a graveside offering or planting (a Roman tradition); as an expression of sorrow for the death of a child (a Saxon tradition); or as a symbol of one who died while sacrificing for others (a Christian tradition)
- Rosemary for remembrance
- Rue as an expression of grief and sorrow

Treatments from Trees

MATERIALS:

Tree bark, wood, bark extracts, tree oils, saps, resins, flower oils, tinctures, or seeds chosen from among the trees listed in the activity

Many familiar healing herbs come from the buds, inner bark, roots, and leaves of trees. Tree barks sometimes contain potent compounds that can be toxic if used improperly or in excess. **Always seek the advice of a trained herbalist before using herbal medicinals.**

Here is a sampling of some of the more common arboreal herbs, including their sources and uses.

Acacia *(Acacia senegal)*: Gum (sap), which is also called gum arabic, is used to moisten, soften, and cleanse the skin.

Bay *(Laurus nobilis)*: Leaves and their essential oil heal and strengthen mental resolve, promote wisdom and honor, and improve digestion.

Birch, yellow *(Betula alleghaniensis)* and black or sweet birch *(B. lenta)*: Tea extract from boiled twigs and inner bark is used as an astringent and as a wintergreen-flavored mouthwash. Tea also makes an effective diuretic and is used to treat diarrhea, rheumatism, and intestinal worms. Sap from these two birches, especially that of the black birch, can be collected in springtime with taps and buckets and boiled down to create a sweet drink.

Cedar, northern white, or arbor vitae *(Thuja occidentalis)*: Cedar massage oil promotes balance and spiritual well-being and strengthens the immune system. **(Not for internal use.)**

Cinnamon bark *(Cinnamomum verum)*: Scent of the inner bark and essential oil attract love and prosperity. Cinnamon also aids digestion, improves appetite, and relieves gas. **(Do not use medicinally when pregnant.)**

(continued on next page)

Clove *(Syzygium aromaticum)*: Essential oil is distilled from the handpicked flower buds, which are also dried to make cloves. As a spiritual essence, clove provides protection and inspires courage. Clove oil is a strong antiseptic. A drop or two applied directly on the gums helps to alleviate toothache.

Elm, slippery *(Ulmus rubra)*: The inner bark is used to make a tea that coats and soothes the throat and stomach. It also helps ease gas, heartburn, and diarrhea.

Eucalyptus *(Eucalyptus globulus)*: Essential oil is used for spiritual purification. Eucalyptus is well known as a treatment for symptoms of the common cold and respiratory problems such as nasal congestion and bronchitis.

Frankincense *(Boswellia species)*: Resin is burned as incense to strengthen and renew faith. Aromatherapy oil is distilled from resin to help reduce stress and promote relaxation.

Myrrh *(Commiphora myrrha)*: When warmed in the sun, the scent of the resin that exudes from the myrrh tree protects from bad thoughts and words and negative spiritual energy. Tincture of myrrh resin strengthens the immune system and helps heal wounds and treat infections, especially those of the mouth and throat.

Nutmeg *(Myristica fragrans)*: This popular spice stimulates psychic energy. Essential oil of nutmeg is used with massage to ease aches and pains. A small amount of this spice, made from the powdered seeds, relieves gas and indigestion. Use sparingly.

Sandalwood *(Santalum album)*: Burn sandalwood as incense to heighten spiritual awareness and when making a wish. Oil distilled from the wood and bark is used in aromatherapy for calming nerves and as an antiseptic.

Willow *(Salix species)*: To the ancient Hebrews, willow was a symbol of loss and mourning. It is also associated with love, both found and forsaken. Wood of the magic wand, willow was also a sacred tree to four Greek goddesses associated with death: Circes, Hecate, Persephone, and Hera. The dried, powdered bark contains salicylates, which are metabolized into salicylic acid (aspirin). Tea made from dried willow bark is a painkiller and anti-inflammatory, but it does not irritate the stomach like aspirin does.

Pillow of Peace and Protection

MATERIALS:

2 pieces muslin cloth (each 7 inches square)

Needle and thread

2 cups dried herbs chosen from those listed in the activity

2 pieces medium to heavy cotton fabric (each 8 inches square)

Health does not just happen; it requires that we listen and respond to our body, mind, and spirit. Because of the hectic lifestyles that many people lead, one of our most commonly neglected needs is that of simple rest and relaxation. Here's how to create a small, portable herbal pillow on which to place your head when it is time to rest.

1. Place the two pieces of muslin cloth together and hem three sides with needle and thread. Turn this inside out.
2. Fill the liner with the herbs you desire (see below) and sew the fourth side closed.
3. Choose a medium to heavy cotton fabric with a design that you find pleasing. Use this to sew a cover for the pillow.
4. Place this herbal pillow underneath the regular pillow you sleep on each night.

Deep rest requires a sense of well-being that is promoted by feelings of safety and solace. Depending on the scents you prefer and the virtues you want your pillow to impart, choose from among the following herbs for your pillow:

- Agrimony to protect from evil while you rest. The yellow flowers smell like apricots.
- Bergamot flowers for serenity and rest
- Chamomile flowers as a sedative and sleep aid, as well as for obtaining energy in times of adversity. The apple-scented yellow flower centers contain the active ingredients.
- Clove for protection and courage

- Fennel to help cure insomnia
- Hops to encourage peacefulness and sleep
- Jasmine for calming and protection
- Lavender as a sedative and cure for insomnia
- Marjoram for inner peace
- Mint for protection and healing
- Sandalwood for relaxation

Herbs for
Aesthetics, Spirit, and Virtue

Anise	Jasmine
Basil	Lavender
Bay	Marjoram
Borage	Mint
Cardamom	Musk
Chamomile	Myrtle
Chicory	Narcissus
Cinnamon	Olive
Citron	Orange
Clove	Rose
Coriander	Saffron
Frankincense	Sandalwood
Ginger	Tamarind
Hyacinth	Thyme
Hyssop	Violet

2

OF AESTHETICS, SPIRIT, AND VIRTUE

I come into my garden,
my sister, my promised bride,
I gather my myrrh and balsam,
I eat my honey and my honeycomb,
I drink my wine and my milk.
Eat, friends, and drink,
drink deep my dearest friends.

—Song of Songs 5:1

Each day, when I go out to work in the garden, I am greeted by a circle of herbs, beaded with dew and radiant with the sun. Joe-Pye weed towers in the center, surrounded by the waist-high, woolly leaves of tansy and grading down to the smallest of thymes along the edge. Every plant has a certain character that I have come to know, borne of flower color, suppleness of stem, and shape of leaf. Each expresses itself in the scent offered at the slightest touch. And there they await me at the dawn.

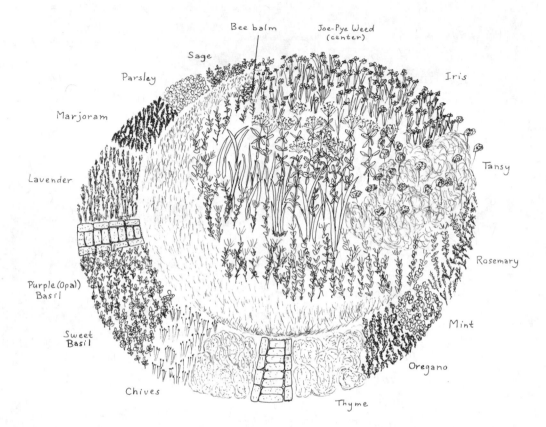

An herb garden planted for scent, taste, and a pleasing composition of colors, textures, and heights. Note the tallest Joe-Pye weed in the center, surrounded by (moving sunwise from the top) iris, tansy, and bee balm (bergamot), a hummingbird favorite.

In the early years, I cultivated herbs for their delicious flavors. But my time among them has drawn me deeper into their world, to a greater understanding of how herbs can lend a fullness to life. Herbs have become an elixir for my spirit, their scents a balm for a harried soul. There are few things more pleasurable than taking a stroll to explore the aesthetic pleasures of herbs, to discover how their virtues can inform and enlighten our spiritual lives.

Even after thirty years of gardening, I still perceive herbs to be alive with beauty and sensory surprises. In the cool of a Vermont morning, I find the garden refreshed. Nibbling the young leaves of basil and tasting their rich layers of flavor tinged with an essence of anise, brushing the delicate leaves of coriander to release their powerful aroma, I understand how herbs have inspired music and poetry ranging from the elegiac to the sublime. The scents of herbs are as layered and complex as the soil from which they spring. Just as my ears register a fraction of any bird's song, my nose strains to detect the subtle perfumes that surround me. Perhaps herbs are loved by so many people because they feed our beings in ways that we are at a loss to explain.

> *In nature, God established humankind, in power.*
>
> *We are dressed in the scaffold of creation: in seeing to recognize all the world in hearing—to understand in smelling—to discover in tasting—to nurture in touching—to govern.*
>
> *In this way, humankind comes to know God, for God is the author of all Creation.*
>
> —Hildegard of Bingen

I slowly make my way around the circle, recalling the history in these herbs spread before me. Long ago, basil was found growing outside the tomb after the resurrection of Jesus Christ. Oil derived from the same thyme that grows in my garden was an essential preservative in the embalming fluid of the Egyptians. Mint, once used for protection and strength, was placed on the floors of Hebrew temples. Sweet marjoram is aptly known for a scent that evokes happiness, but coriander, with its bold and delightful touch of freshness, has somehow come to represent modesty and merit. And sage, an herb that possesses the virtue of its own namesake, wisdom, also engenders good health and long life.

These are some herbs that speak to me through eye, nose, and hand. Herbs communicate in powerful ways if we attune our senses to their language.

HERB GARDENS FOR THE SPIRIT

Beloved Hildegard, whose monastic spirit blossomed along the Rhine during the twelfth century, was part of an awakening to creation and spirit that radiated across the world in word and deed, song, dance, and image. At about the same time, Islamic gardens were unfurling their greenery as symbols of spiritual awakening. In his groundbreaking book *Kitab al-Filaha,* or *The Book of Agriculture,* which was completed in 1180 CE, the author Ibn al-Awwam showed the virtues of growing plants for food and medicine and as a way of asking for God's blessing, particularly plants that are good for the human heart—orange, rose, and basil. Long sections of the *Kitab* expound on the aesthetics of color and scent.

Islamic gardens were often enclosed—a symbolic image of the universe where sense and spirit intertwined. In these quiet spaces, sensory experiences enlivened the imagination. Pools of water formed the center of these worlds that revealed the depths of creation's mysteries and reflected our own place in the cosmos. Sitting in a pavilion set as a gemstone in the center of the garden ring, generations of Muslims sat beneath the stars, seeking communion with the Creator, even as scents of the nocturnal, aromatic *Chandni*, or moonflower, and other fragrant blossoms, healed and made them whole.

The branches of the Tūbā tree,
the tongue reciting the Koran,
the roses there in Paradise,
their fragrance is Allah, Allah.

—Yunus Emre, fourteenth century

Ibn Sina, a medieval Islamic herbalist and author of *Kitab al-Shifa,* or *Book of Healing,* and whose work is the basis of today's Yunani medicine, believed that emotion is influenced by the quality of our environment—that fragrances can strengthen and enliven both heart and spirit, or *Ruh.* The promise of Yunani medicine, which dates back to tenth-century Persia, is that disease can be treated by restoring the body's four humors—blood, phlegm, yellow bile, and black bile—to their rightful balance. The humors are associated with temperament. Sina spoke of four chief emotions that rest at the opposing ends of two continua: joy and sorrow, fear and anger. Fragrances, said Sina, help us experience life as joyful and refreshing. Powerful scents can lead to a life in which our bodies and spirits exist in a state of healthful balance and exhilaration, which he called *mufarrih*.

Ibn Sina believed lavender, with its passionate purple blossoms, is among the most influential fragrances that can cleanse and enliven our hearts and spirits. It is as refreshing as any floral scent. The name of this native of the western Mediterranean comes from the Latin *lavandus*, "to be washed."

Other herbs that emanate a potent, pleasing essence include sandalwood, with its power to impart spiritual awareness; rose, with its healing nature; fragrant saffron; calming cinnamon; and the yellow-flowered cardamom, attractor of love.

OF SENSES AND VIRTUES

Using herbs and flowers to express and encourage desired emotional states and to instill virtues is a tradition that dates back to ancient Persia. It grew out of folklore and myth and the natural associations that human experience began to discover with particular herbs and flowers. The herbal "Language of Flowers" evolved in Victorian England and became widely used.

My herb garden was planned with all of the senses in mind. The tall and open purple panicles of Joe-Pye weed in the center are surrounded by red and purple bergamots, or bee balms, with tubular petals that hummingbirds find irresistible. One whiff of its spicy flowers imbues a feeling of serenity. Sun-like florets of tansy and its soft, woolly, fern-like leaves, with their powerful, pungent scent radiating in the late-day sun, bring to mind the deep healing that comes from strong medicine. Arching white tapers of gooseneck loosestrife intermingle with the canary-like flower heads of yellow iris.

The outer circle is a riot of colors, textures, and scents. Bending down, I can reach a bouquet of basils that paint a leafy collage that smells of India, their exotic homeland. From the deep green of sweet basil to the pale hues of lemon and the brilliant leaves of opal basil that grows near the apex of the herb garden where the brick path intersects with the wider world—these are the scents that calm the spirit and foster balance within. To the Hindus of the sixteenth century, basil was an herb that emanated the scent of love. Brides wore their long hair plaited in bands and adorned with floral crowns of hyacinth and basil intertwined with musk and its penetrating, irresistible, amorous draw.

What mysterious internal connection causes scent to be the strongest aspect of our sensory perception that triggers memory?

Scent is our emotional mnemonic. Recollections of the heart come flooding back at the faintest whiff of a flower that may have wafted on an evening breeze many years ago as we shared a first kiss. Sweet rosewater, with its tincture of romance and longing, transports us to places beyond and into an ethereal realm that floats above the tribulations of our daily doldrums. The thirteenth-century Christian mystic Meister Eckhart truly captured the essence of rose when he wrote, "This I know. The only way to live is like the rose, which lives without a why."

The season is coming
when the birds will sing
and the turtle dove's cooing
will be heard in our land;
green figs will ripen on the trees
and blossoming vines
will fill the air with their fragrance.

—Song of Songs 2:12–13

Medieval monks believed that appreciation of nature, even smelling the sweet scent of a flower, was good for both body and soul. Perfume was considered such a permeating essence of the human spirit that the word comes from the Latin *per* and *fumus*, "through smoke." A sixteenth-century Benedictine friar, Louis of Blois, or "Blosins," believed that the pleasures of nature bring our spirits closer to God. "May the beauty of flowers and other creatures draw the heart to love and admire God, their creator," wrote Blosins. "The birds sing the praise of God in heaven so that man may learn to praise Him in his heart."

Fragrance is more than an aesthetic; it is one aspect of the intersection between sensory perception and ethics, between beauty and truth. That which elevates our pleasurable experience with the wonders of creation also instills a desire to transform that sensory delight into the goodness of a life well lived. Fragrance opens our hearts and lifts our spirits; it inspires us to attain an equilibrium in which there is no incongruity between the olfactory bliss of a flower and the good will that we spread among those who enter within the reaches of our own emanation. "To a person of good will," wrote Hildegard of Bingen, "God will grant what is asked, as the will to good is the sweetest of all aromas."

A Wreath of Pure Beauty

MATERIALS:

Wire wreath frame or a circle woven from grapevine about 12 inches in diameter

12 sprigs each hyssop, lavender, and myrtle that are 6 inches long

24-gauge floral wire

Cutting pliers

Dried flowers

Herbs of your choice: rose, jasmine, violet, orange peel, or cinnamon sticks

Why are wreaths so popular when we celebrate holidays of the spirit? What is a crown if not a small wreath adorning one's head? Wreaths are a symbol of the circle that connects us all—the shape of simplicity, without beginning or end. They call to mind the cycles of the seasons. A single wreath can also join with another circle to link and form the symbol of infinity.

Hyssop and lavender are classic herbal symbols of cleanliness, clarity of vision, and purity of spirit. The Hebrew word *ezob*, or "holy herb," may be the root of hyssop's name. In Roman mythology, sprigs of myrtle are a gift from Venus and a sign of her beauty. Lavender and myrtle draw love to the one who understands their meaning.

1. Use a wire wreath frame or a circle woven from a grapevine, 12 inches in diameter, as the base for a wreath. Lay out 24 sprigs each of hyssop, lavender, and myrtle. Cut each sprig to about 6 inches.

2. Take fine wire (24-gauge floral wire will do) and use it to wrap and fasten the end of each sprig along the wreath frame, alternating among each of the three kinds of herbs as you progress. Align the sprigs so they are all facing in the same direction and angled slightly toward the outside of the frame.

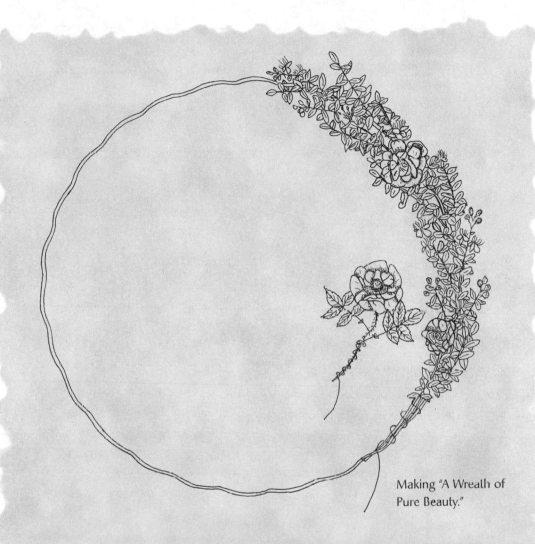

Making "A Wreath of Pure Beauty."

3. When the basic wreath is complete, cut about twelve 6-inch pieces of wire—one for each dried flower and the other adornments you will attach to the wreath. For each item, twist the end of a piece of wire around the stem or tip and wrap the other end of the wire around the wreath frame. Use dried rose blossoms for beauty, jasmine flowers for admirable qualities, violets for loyalty, dried orange peel for joy and abundance, or cinnamon sticks for calmness and good spirits. All five of these herbs also attract love. Tuck the flowers down into the wreath of herbs

(continued on next page)

and alternate between each kind of flower as you work around the circle.

4. When the wreath is completed, hang it in a bright place, but not in direct sunlight.

As a variation on this activity, weave a small, simpler head wreath and wear it as a blessing of purity, joy, love, and abundance.

Sachets of Courage

MATERIALS:

> *Scissors*
>
> *1 yard green or yellow light cotton cloth*
>
> *Plate about 8 inches in diameter (template)*
>
> *Fabric chalk to trace circle*
>
> *One handful each bay leaves and the dried leaves and flowers of borage and thyme*
>
> *Small bowl*
>
> *1 teaspoon whole cloves*
>
> *2–3 drops ginger oil*
>
> *Colored yarn*

We cannot grow without a willingness to let go of our old selves. In both Christianity and Sufism, fear is considered a significant obstacle that we must overcome in order to clear a path for spiritual growth. We need to let down our defenses, to let go of our baggage and prepare for a new journey into the unknown mysteries of the spirit.

Which aromatic herbs will help us embrace newness and uncertainty? Ginger, bay, borage, and thyme impart courage and strength. Clove lends courage as well as protection. Keep these herbs close by with sachets of courage, which are small and can be carried wherever you go.

1. Cut several 8-inch circles of light cotton cloth that is colored with shades of green (peace and hope) and/or yellow (happiness and excitement). Use an 8-inch plate and fabric chalk to trace the template onto the cloth.

2. Crumble a handful of some bay leaves plus the same amount of dried leaves and flowers of borage and thyme into a small bowl. Mix in 1 teaspoon of whole cloves. Add a few drops of ginger oil and stir well. Let the mixture sit for 10 minutes while the oil soaks into the herbs and flowers.

(continued on next page)

3. Drop heaping tablespoons of the mixture into the center of each circle of cloth. Pull the edges of each circle up and around the mixture, creating a small, tight pouch that encloses the herbs. Gather the edges together and tie with yarn to complete each sachet.

4. Place the sachets in locations where you will have access to them throughout the day, such as next to your bed, in the car, in your briefcase, and in your purse. Take time to focus on your faith at different times of the day. During each of these reflections, and especially when you feel afraid or threatened or when the trials of life cause your faith to waiver, pick up one of the sachets and inhale the scents of strength, courage, and protection from fear and doubt.

Bathing Balm

MATERIALS:

Herbal teas (3–4 teabags) or
Essential oils (6–12 drops) of your choice or
2 handfuls/1 cup loose dried herbs
Tea ball or strainer or
Cheesecloth and string

NOTE: This activity offers several alternatives for preparing herbal baths. Choose the specific method you want to use before obtaining the materials.

To take a bath is to clean; to bathe is to immerse yourself in a world of scent and sensual pleasure that heals body and spirit. Soak as the steam and aroma of one or more of these herbs wafts over you:

- Basil for love, purification, good fortune, protection from harm, and refreshment of a tired mind
- Sandalwood to relax
- Marjoram to relieve soreness, ease tension, and encourage sleep
- Chamomile to bring comfort, peace, and sleep

Although sweet, apple-scented chamomile is known for its properties to soothe, Egyptians associated the yellow heart of its flower with the sun and, therefore, its ability to provide energy and initiative when under duress. An old tradition in the Greek Orthodox Church was to use basil to help purify holy water. But beware its power to hold one to the truth: courts in India once required people to swear an oath over a sprig of basil!

1. Herbal baths can be prepared by adding to the water either herbal oils or an infusion of herbal teas. About 6 to 12 drops of herbal oil will do for a normal-sized bath. If you are using packaged herbal teas, fill the tub and soak 3 or 4 teabags of each herb

(continued on next page)

you want to include. You can also use a tea ball containing loose tea. Another method is to create an infusion of each herb and add that to the bath. Put 2 handfuls of dried herbs into a small pot of boiling water and steep for 15 minutes. Then pour this solution through a strainer and add it to the bathwater. Alternatively, you can tie about 1 cup of dried herbs into a pouch made of a cheesecloth with the four corners pulled up and cinched together with string to form a small bag. As you fill the tub, run the water over this herbal bag, then hang it from the spout and let it soak.

2. While you are basking in the herbal bath and breathing in the vapor rich with herbal essence, you may want to read or recite the following poem that I have written, or another meaningful prayer:

CREATOR—
That my face will bloom
and shine joy to all I meet;
That my skin will catch
the warmth and light of the sun;
That my hands will extend
toward others as I grow;
That I will take root
in my community;
That I will find strength
to speak truth in the world;
That my life will return
the love I have received;
That I will nurture Earth
for those who are yet to come.

Soap for the Spirit

MATERIALS:

Molds (optional)

2 bars pure unscented glycerin soap (cannot contain any stabilizers) or the bulk kind found in craft stores

Cheese grater

5–7 teaspoons finely ground herbs or 15–20 drops herbal essential oil: calendula, mint, or hyssop

Coffee grinder or food processor

Double boiler

Spoon

OPTIONAL (FOR HOMEMADE MOLDS): Aluminum foil, shapes for molds, scallop or clam shell, dab of almond oil or olive oil.

We wash our hands to keep our skin clean and healthy and to prevent the spread of disease. Why don't we wash our spirits to heal them and keep them pure? Meld one or more of these herbs into soap so that you can partake of their virtues each time you wash:

- Calendula, with its relaxing floral scent, has leaves and flowers that cleanse and detoxify. Oil from its flower petals is an antiseptic for wounds and sores and is often used for skin treatments with aromatherapy. Hindus use sprigs and flowers of calendula to beautify their temples.
- Mints are well known for their cleansing, antiseptic properties. The essence of peppermint energizes a tired spirit and inspires one to be polite and kind. Spearmint imparts kindness and warm feelings toward others.
- Hyssop, with its aromatic leaves, is cited throughout the Bible for its power of spiritual cleansing and for its ability to purify those who are sick.

(continued on next page)

1. Making herbal soap is easy. First, decide whether you want to pour the soap into molds or make small balls of soap. If you're going to use soap molds, keep them handy. You can create your own molds by doubling-up a piece of aluminum foil and pressing it into a form. Or, use a seashell for a mold and coat the inside with a touch of olive or almond oil.

2. Take 2 bars or chunks of pure, unscented glycerin soap and grate them coarsely.

3. Choose the herbs you want to use and work them in a coffee grinder or food processor until you have 5 to 7 tablespoons that are finely ground. Instead of dried herbs you can substitute a *total* of 15–20 drops of herbal essential oils.

4. Melt the grated soap in a double boiler, stirring occasionally, and blend in the dried herbs or drops of herbal oils.

5. When this is stirred to consistency, pour it immediately into the molds. Or let it cool for about 15 minutes, then spoon out some golfball-sized dollops and roll them into spheres. Note: If soap does not melt in 10 minutes, it may contain stabilizers and will not melt.

6. In a dark, dry space, let the soap cure for about 2 weeks before using. Then you can cleanse your spirit every time you wash your hands.

A Light of Life

MATERIALS:

Several 8-inch-long unscented soy wax candles with long wicks

Old Popsicle sticks or pieces of twig of similar length

Scissors

String

Coffee grinder or mortar and pestle;

½ cup (total) finely ground frankincense, anise, or sandalwood (or a mix) or 1 ounce herbal oil(s)

2 tube-shaped potato chip containers;

Large saucepan

10-inch-deep pan of water at room temperature

Double boiler

Paint-stirring stick

1 pound unscented flaked soy wax

Cooking thermometer

One of your favorite inspirational books

Optional (if candlewick is short): Needle and thread

Light shows us the way; it illuminates the path so that we do not become lost. Our inner light can be fed by breathing the scents of herbs as they are released in a flame. In smoke, the flame reduces these virtues to their most fundamental essences so that they can blend with our body and spirit. Our inner light is fed by the single, dancing flame of a candle.

Any number of herbal scents can be incorporated into your candle. The three herbs suggested here are chosen for their potency, pleasing aroma, and virtuous qualities. They were commonly used in ancient gardens, ranging from the Islamic gardens of Persia to the cloistered medieval gardens of Europe.

(continued on next page)

- Frankincense clears the mind's eye and improves inner vision. It emanates a pure, rejuvenating spiritual essence that enhances meditation even as it offers protection from influences that would work counter to your spiritual growth and awareness.
- Anise is an exotic herb from Greece, Egypt, and Asia Minor. The oil from anise seeds is uplifting, promotes centering, and encourages good dreams.
- Sandalwood relieves stress and anxiety, relaxes, and—some believe—helps grant wishes.

1. Start with a plain, unscented soy or beeswax candle about 8 inches long. Compared to oil-based paraffin wax, soy wax and beeswax are made from a renewable resource, burn longer, and produce less soot. Soy wax can be cleaned up with soap and water.

2. Gather together some old Popsicle sticks or twigs of about equivalent length. Cut some pieces of string about 1 foot long. Tie the end of each piece of string onto a Popsicle stick or twig, and the other end onto the wick of a candle. Use the stick as a "handle" for holding and dipping each candle. If the candlewick is too short to tie, run a needle and thread through the wick and knot it around the wick. Tie the thread onto a Popsicle stick or twig and hold this as you dip the candle.

3. Using a coffee grinder or mortar and pestle, prepare ½ cup of a finely ground mix of the herb, or herbs that you choose. Alternatively, have the scented herbal oil at hand.

4. Without soaking the cardboard, carefully wipe clean 2 round, tube-shaped potato chip containers and stand up one of these (empty) in the middle of a large saucepan. Place another pan holding a potato chip can full of cold water next to the first chip container.

5. Using a double boiler, melt 1 pound of soy wax. Stir in ½ cup of ground herb(s) or 6 drops (total) of the herbal oils until the mixture is uniform. When adding dried herbs to the melted wax, allow it to steep on the heat for an hour at 180°F, stirring occa-

sionally. This will enable the scent and essence of the herbs to enter the wax.

6. Carefully pour this melted, herbal wax into the empty chip container.

7. Dip one of the tapered candles into the liquid wax until it is completely coated, then dip the candle into the cold water and hold it there for a few seconds to harden this first layer. Stir the wax occasionally with the paint stick so that the herbs do not settle to the bottom. Alternate dipping the candle into the hot wax and cold water until you build up a layer of herbal wax that is about $\frac{1}{8}$-inch thick. Make sure that the wax builds up evenly on all sides of the candle. Dip the candle one last time into the cold water and hang it by the wick until it has cooled and hardened.

8. Later, while you are appreciating the scent of your lit candle, your light of life, read a favorite book that inspires you, one that will take you on an inner journey to connect with your own inner light, and to discover how it intersects with the manifold lights of creation.

ALTERNATIVE: Begin with only a wick and use the same waxing and cooling procedure to form an entire candle.

Herbs for
Feeding the Spirit and Giving Thanks

Basil
Bay
Borage
Cardamom
Chili
Chives
Cinnamon
Citron
Clove
Coriander
Cornflower
Cumin
Delphinium
Dill
Eucalyptus
Fennel
Frankincense
Garlic
Ginger
Hibiscus
Horseradish

Hyssop
Jasmine
Larkspur
Lavendar
Leeks
Lotus
Mint
Miswak
Myrtle
Orange
Oregano
Palm
Parsley
Patchouli
Pepper, black
Poppy (red)
Romaine
  lettuce
Rose
Rosemary
Rosewater

Saffron
Sage
Savory
Star anise
Sunflower
Sweetfern
Sweetgrass
Tansy
Thyme
Tobacco
Turmeric
Verbena
Violet
Wild
  marjoram
Wild thyme
Willow
Wormwood
Yarrow

3

FEEDING THE SPIRIT, GIVING THANKS

God appeared as a rainbow and said to Ezekiel:
"Son of man, eat what is given to you;
eat this scroll, then go and speak
    to the House of Israel."
I opened my mouth;
    he gave me the scroll to eat and said,
"Son of man, feed and be satisfied by the scroll
    I am giving you.
I ate it and it tasted sweet as honey."

                                  —Ezekiel 3:1–3

The adage "you are what you eat" can be viewed in different ways. The obvious meaning is that the food we consume is digested and absorbed; it becomes part of our bodies down to the cellular level. From the perspective of emotion and contentment, our feelings of health and fulfillment reflect the quality of our meals. The goodness inherent in food emanates from the pleasant scents and flavors of herbs and the resulting sense of satiety. At the spiritual level, every time we eat we help cocreate our body, and our self, with God. Herbs that we eat can

Some popular herbs for holiday meals (left to right): rosemary, parsley, and garlic.

have a profound effect on every level of our being, and so, too, our relationships with God and other people.

Food is also a major force that binds our families together. When my paternal grandmother, Annina, was seventeen years old, she was sent to the United States aboard an ocean liner. She did not want to go, but passage had been bought at great expense for her older sister, who had subsequently fallen in love and refused to leave Italy. So Annina's father looked at her and said, "You are going to America." Among the belongings that arrived in her enormous "steamer" trunk were many traditional family recipes for everything from breads to biscuits and pies to pastries.

I cannot imagine what Easter would have been without Grandma's signature seasonal dishes, including *Pasticcio Carnevale di Pasqua (Pasticcio Rustica)*, Easter Carnival (Rustic) Pie. Three cheeses, sweet Italian sausage, prosciutto, eggs, and just the right touch of parsley and black pepper combined to create a rich flavor that was an essential part of our celebration of springtime and the Easter renewal.

Christmas Eve was another occasion when we shared traditional Italian dishes. One of my favorites was the meal of codfish, *baccalà*. Although *baccalà* really refers to "dried cod," we used the fresh, tender filets that were available to us where we lived on the New England coast. Zestfully seasoned with herbs—parsley, oregano, garlic, and black pepper—the filets filled the house with a hearty aroma as they baked with olive oil and potatoes. On many a Christmas Eve, when Grandma had been busy baking her mouthwatering Italian cookies and pastries, my mother, Esther, would prepare the *baccalà* and bring it to the feast.

As children, the long wait for our delicious evening meal on December 24th was excruciating, but the experience served to heighten our anticipation of the magic that awaited us on Christmas morning. Sometimes, my father, Ralph, would ask Grandma to say grace, and she always seemed to remember what was one of her own fondest parts of Christmas: celebrating the *Bambino Piccolo*, the "little baby," Jesus.

Years later, the scents of these particular herbs evoke memories of those early family gatherings as we continue to celebrate the two major religious events of our faith. The setting and seating arrangement help reinforce our sense of community as well as the honor and respect in which elders are regarded, who often sit at the "head" of the table. The smells, tastes, and even appearance of each platter of food reveal that the entire aspect of these meals is purposeful and spiritual. This confluence of worldly delights and ethereal excitement enriches our lives and feeds us, body and soul. These rituals are guideposts that remind us of what is truly important in life.

FOOD AND SPIRIT

In a thousand ways since childhood, I have come to understand that *what* we eat and *how* we eat are signs of our physical health and spiritual wholeness. The Jewish tradition is particularly rich in beliefs and practices relating to food, faith, and community. In the Zoharic Kabbalah, which dates back to late thirteenth-century Spain, our bodies are vessels of divinity. Arguably the greatest single book of Jewish mysticism, the Zohar teaches that in the act of eating we cocreate our bodies with the Divine. Food is a gift from the Divine, and eating is a way of inviting the Divine body into our physical self and nourishing our spirits. And like Ezekiel, who eats the very scroll on which God offers the wisdom of prophecy, when we eat with spiritual intent, we consume the word of God (Ezekiel 3:1–3).

Some medieval Jewish mystics were herbalists who drew on their knowledge of the natural world and divine wisdom to heal others. According to Zoharic teaching, our bodies grow according to the food we eat, and we are molded by our own spiritual actions. In order to obtain food, we must destroy the lives of plants and animals. Both cocreation and destruction are sacred acts, deserving of our respect and reverence. The relationship between what we eat and who we become was made clear in the Garden of Eden:

> You may eat from every tree in the garden,
> but not from the Tree of the Knowledge of
>   Good and Evil;
> for on the day that you eat from it,
> you will surely die.
>
> *—Genesis 2:16–17*

Belief in the spiritual nature of our relationship with food is a common theological thread that courses through many traditions. Cistercian monks eat one main meal each day, which includes only bread, vegetables, herbs, and beans. In the Torah, wine and bread had special symbolic value in Israelite ritual. At the end of each day of fasting and worship during the month of Ramadan, Muslims share *Iftar* meals and partake of foods that were once consumed by the prophet Muhammad to help with fasting. These include hibiscus flowers, essence of rosewater, and dates. Afterward, teeth are cleaned by brushing with a *miswak*, the frayed end of a root from a shrubby tree *(Salvadora persica)*, which has been soaked in rosewater. *Miswak* roots produce substances that have been shown to help kill harmful mouth bacteria and prevent the accumulation of plaque. Rosewater sweetens the breath, lifts spirits, and helps with digestion.

JUDAIC TRADITIONS

Jewish cooking from different regions and time periods has incorporated herbs in different ways. Spicy Sephardic cooking originated with Jews living in Sephard, the Iberian Peninsula of Portugal and Spain. Many dishes are prepared with olive oil and seasoned with strong herbs: turmeric, cumin, cinnamon, ginger, saffron, chili, and garlic. Cooking among Ashkenazic (a Hebrew word for Germany) Jews uses a great variety of herbs and is known for its "sweet and sour" stews. The rich and diverse meals of Israeli cooking incorporate foods, herbs, and dishes from around the world—from wherever people have come to settle in the homeland.

When the tribes of Israel fled from bondage in Egypt, they lived in desert exile for forty years. God provided them with bread from heaven. "The manna looked like coriander seed, the color of gum resin. The people went about collecting it, ground it up in hand-mills or pounded it in mortars, then boiled it in the pot and made it into cakes. It tasted like butter-cakes. When dew fell on the camp at night, the manna fell with it" (Numbers 11:7–10). Still, people lamented the cost of freedom. "Think of the fish we used to eat free in Egypt, the cucumbers, melons, leeks, onions and garlic! Here we are wasting away, stripped of everything; there is nothing but manna for us to look at!" (Numbers 11:5–6). Manna was the generosity of God's spirit descended from heaven.

In the Zohar, giving to those in need is done with a generous spirit, taking joy in the act of helping others. It is a reminder that giving to the less fortunate is one of the two most important qualities of our life for which we will be judged after death, along with study of the Torah. In this ethical tradition, the volume of food we take is not to be more than we need. Coriander is associated with the virtue of providing for others who are in need. Its Hebrew name comes from *gemul dalim*, "beneficence to the lowly."

When they measured in an Omer
  what they had gathered,
the man who had gathered more
  had not too much,
the man who had gathered less had not too little.
Each found he had gathered what he needed.

Exodus 16:17–18

Herbs are an organic connection between the vital earth and the long Jewish history of living close to nature. Forty years of exile in the desert helped mold the rituals and ceremonies of faith: listening to the tent flapping in the wind, foraging and hunting for food, searching for water, stepping away from the cooking fires at night to gaze up into a star-filled dome. Herbal traditions lend a richness and depth, a life and energy to foods eaten during the many Jewish holy days.

Ritual cleansing of the hands before eating bread is said to alleviate one's suffering (Zohar Hadash 86d–87a Midrash Ruth). Hands must be clean. Purity is essential if a blessing is to be given and received.

Purify me with hyssop
until I am clean;
wash me until
I am whiter than snow.

—Psalms 51:7

Passover marks a transformation from a century of time during which the ancient Israelites lived as separate tribes enslaved in Egypt, to a time of challenge and freedom as a nation together, wandering in the wilderness. Pesach, or Passover, marks this call, this journey to redemption. Moses was a true prophet who heard God and led his people out of Egypt. In Hebrew, the word *prophet* is *navee*, "seer of visions."

During the flight from Egypt, there was no time to wait for bread dough to rise, so unleavened flatbread, called matzah, was baked and eaten. Today, unleavened bread is eaten during the Seder meal and throughout Passover. Eating unleavened bread is a pathway to gaining knowledge, to joining with the Divine.

Bitter herbs, *maror,* are consumed during the Seder: a small amount of romaine lettuce and horseradish, and sometimes chives and parsley. Eating bitter herbs is a reminder of the generations of suffering in Egypt. The bitter taste of these herbs also helps one empathize with the suffering of others and engenders, in an open heart, a desire for kindness and mercy, *rachamim*.

Maror is placed on the Seder plate, which includes the other Passover symbols, to remind us of the importance of mercy in our lives. The Seder ritual—retelling the story of deliverance, the meal and the songs of joy and celebration—are also part of God's plan for strengthening covenants with people of faith. Food is the blessing consumed to enrich our spirits; song and prayer are the offering returned.

The taste of bitter herbs is tempered by the pleasant flavor of *charoset*, a Seder side dish of fruit and nuts spiced with cinnamon and, sometimes, ginger. *Charoset* has its roots in the Hebrew word *cheres,* meaning "clay." The thick fruit symbolizes the mortar that was used to lay stone and brick during the time in Egypt. Cinnamon sticks represent the straw that was harvested to construct the walls of Pharaoh's elaborate edifices. The sweet taste of *charoset* is a ray of hope in the midst of hardship.

> *That night, the flesh is to be eaten,*
> *roasted over the fire;*
> *it must be eaten with unleavened bread*
> *and bitter herbs.*
>
> —Exodus 12:8–9

Another rich Jewish herbal tradition is part of the Havdalah ceremony. Each week on Saturday evening, Shabbat comes to a close when the stars appear in the sky. Havdalah, which comes from the Hebrew *l'havdeel,* meaning "to separate" or "to distinguish," marks this transition from a day of rest to the days of work that follow.

At the end of Shabbat, a small, ornately decorated container is filled with sweet, fragrant herbs, often cinnamon, cloves, and cardamom. Bay leaves are occasionally included in the Havdalah spice box. As the box is passed around, each person opens it and inhales the sweet aroma that symbolizes the joys of rest, prayer, and re-creation that are central to Shabbat. Throughout the workweek, the scents of the spice box are opened, and this fragrance evokes both the pleasures of Shabbats passed and the anticipation of those to come.

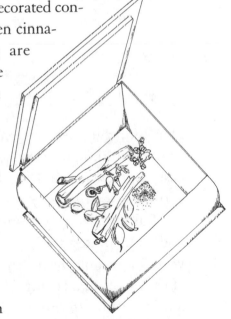

Havdalah spice box containing cinnamon sticks (left & center), cloves (top), and cardamom seedpods (bottom).

GIVING THANKS

Gratitude for our daily blessings is often expressed through herbal rituals.

Some years ago, I was co-leading a canoe trip down the Connecticut River with members of the Abenaki Nation, an indigenous culture of north-ern New England. We paddled over to the riverbank to sample some useful plants that were growing there. As the simple, respectful cere-mony of thanksgiving unfolded, I could see a sudden realization flash in the eyes of the novices who were present, discovering for the first time that they were experiencing another worldview—one in which the nat-ural world is sacred and treated with respect and awe. Novices looked on with reverence as a gift of seeds was shaken from that plant and sown to propagate more of their kind. Then came the symbolic gifts of tobacco and sunflower seeds to complete the circle and restore the bal-ance. Finally, an Abenaki prayer of thanks, *oliwni*, was offered to the four directions, then to Earth and Sky.

In our time, it is easy to lose perspective on the real meaning of grat-itude, which is a way of restoring balance to the relationship between the giver and the receiver. Gifts from the physical realm embody the spirit of generos-ity from the giver. The Jewish festival or holiday of Sukkot, the Feast of the Tabernacles, bears a remarkable resem-blance to the Abenaki thanksgiving ceremony from North America. During Sukkot, four species of herbs are offered to the six directions—east, south, west, and north, and then up to the sky and down to the earth.

> *If the only prayer you say in your entire life is "Thank you," that would suffice.*
>
> —Meister Eckhart

Sukkot, a harvest festival, begins on the fifth day after Yom Kippur and is celebrated for nine days, commemorating the Exodus and forty years of wandering in the desert. It is also called *Chag Ha'Asif*, the "Festival of Ingathering." The first fruits of the harvest are presented at temple as an offering to God in gratitude for the gifts of the harvest. This ritual requires that frankincense be burned as a sacrificial offering. "You shall add oil to it and put frankincense upon it" (Leviticus 2:15–16). Frankincense is a symbol of holiness, respect, and purification.

Daily processions are made in the synagogue during Sukkot. Each is called a *Hoshana*, "please save us," after the central prayer of the procession. The four species of herbs are carried while circling with the Torah, then these herbs are waved in the six directions during the blessing ceremony: *etrog* (citron), *lulav* (palm), *hodas* (myrtle), and *arava* (willow).

CELEBRATIONS AND BLESSINGS

History often refers to the ancient tribes of Israel, as well as Native American tribes and the tribes of Africa. The root of this word is the Latin *tribus*, which was once used to describe any of the three large divisions of the ancient Romans.

What is our tribe today? With whom do we share the table? The world has grown smaller and this has brought us all closer together. In Kabbalah, the Jewish mystical tradition, the eater prepares with intent for the spiritual experience of eating, of sharing with the Divine and with all of the guests at the table. The meal is eaten calmly and reverently, in respect for food as a

> *For God will bless you*
> *in all your harvest*
> *and all your handiwork,*
> *and you will be filled with joy.*
>
> —Deuteronomy 16:15

gift from the Divine. During festivals, however, eating is not a sober experience, but a celebration. "Then you are to feast on all the good things God has given you, you and your household, and with you the Levite and the stranger who lives among you" (Deuteronomy 26:11).

A traditional preparatory prayer asks to receive the gift in a state of grace, *va-yitav libo*, literally "and his heart was joyful." "A good blessing," *berakhah tovah*, comes after eating at least *ke-zayit*, the "volume of an olive." A final blessing is offered when the meal is over and everyone is satisfied.

Easter Carnival (Rustic) Pie and Pepper Biscuits

Easter Carnival (Rustic) Pie
(Pasticcio Carnevale di Pasqua [*Pasticcio Rustica*])

Celebrate Easter with this traditional Italian dish and its flavorful companion, pepper biscuits. The herbs and spices complement one another perfectly. Every Easter, after we had attended Sunday service, our family gathered for a meal in which Easter Carnival Pie, or Rustic Pie, was the centerpiece. In this version of our family recipe, I have added a touch of rosemary, which is symbolic of the resurrection of Christ.

YIELD: 1 large pie

FILLING

½ pound sweet Italian sausage
6 eggs
1 pound ricotta cheese
½ pound prosciutto (cubed)
½ pound mozzarella cheese (cubed)

½ cup grated Parmesan cheese
¼ cup finely chopped parsley
½ teaspoon rosemary
Freshly ground black pepper to taste

PIE CRUST

2 cups flour
½ cup butter, melted
½ teaspoon salt

2 eggs
½ cup milk
Beaten egg yolk (optional)

1. Bake or fry the sausage, then allow it to cool. Chop coarsely and set aside.
2. Make the pie crust *(scorza di pasticcio rustica)*. Mix the flour and butter together. Add the remaining pie crust ingredients and knead the dough a *short* time. Divide into two pieces—one of which is two-thirds of the total. Roll out the larger piece and use it to line a round, deep-sided baking dish, preferably one of glass

or crockery. Roll out the second piece and set it aside. This will become the top crust.

3. Preheat the oven to 400°F.
4. Make the filling by beating the eggs and ricotta cheese together in a large bowl until smooth. Add the remaining ingredients and blend well.
5. Pour this mixture into the baking dish lined with the pie crust shell. Cover with the remaining pie crust. Cut slits in the top crust to allow the steam to escape. If desired, the top may be brushed with one beaten egg yolk to create a sheen.
6. Bake at 400°F for 15 minutes. Reduce the heat to 325°F and bake for another 45 minutes, or longer, until the pie becomes firm in the center. Cool before serving.

Pepper Biscuits (I Biscotti di Pepe) and Pepper Sticks (I Bastone di Pepe)

DOUGH

1 package active dry yeast
1 cup warm water
1 cup oil
1 teaspoon salt

1½ teaspoons coarsely ground black pepper
1½ teaspoons fennel seed
3 to 4 cups flour

YIELD: About 6 dozen 2-inch biscuits or 6-inch sticks

1. Dissolve the yeast in the warm water. Add the oil, salt, pepper, and fennel seed.
2. Add the flour gradually to create a dough that is firm but not too dry. Turn the dough onto a pastry board and knead for about 10 minutes. Let this rise until it doubles in size.
3. Shape the dough into either biscuits or sticks.

PEPPER BISCUITS: Roll the dough into ½-inch-thick ropes and cut these into 6-inch sections. Twist each end in toward the center, as if making a small knot, so that the ends just overlap in the middle. Moisten the ends

(continued on next page)

so they stick together where they meet. Each biscuit will be about 2 inches across.

PEPPER STICKS: Roll the dough out into ropes that are about 6 inches long and ³⁄₈ inch in diameter.

4. Preheat the oven to 400°F. Bring a large pot of water to boil.
5. Carefully drop the biscuits or sticks into the boiling water, a few at a time. At first, they will sink. As they rise to the surface, remove and let them cool on a drain board. You may need to reshape them a bit after they have cooled.
6. Once they have drained, bake the biscuits or sticks on an ungreased cookie sheet for 20 to 25 minutes, until medium brown.

Herbal Easter Eggs

MATERIALS:

> Sewing needle
>
> 12 medium white eggs
>
> Skewer
>
> Bowl
>
> Glass of warm water
>
> Assortment of colorful and interestingly shaped dried
>   flower petals, leaves, and seeds
>
> Clean paper towels
>
> Sharp pencil
>
> White glue

OPTIONAL (FOR MOBILE): 3 pieces of ⅛-inch wooden dowels about 12 inches long, colored yarn, 7 completed Easter eggs, 7 pieces of toothpick that are ½ inch long, and scissors.

1. Use the sharp tip of a sewing needle to carefully make a tiny hole roughly ¹⁄₁₆ inch in size in both ends of an egg. Stick the end of a skewer into the egg and gently swish it around to break up the soft contents while being careful to not crack the shell. Hold the egg over a bowl and blow into the hole on the top (narrow) end of the egg until all of the contents have been emptied. Fill the egg with warm water, then blow it out to wash the inside of the egg. Repeat this washing and allow the egg to dry. Prepare 7 hollow eggshells in this fashion.
2. Gather a collection of colorful dried flower petals, leaves, and seeds of herbs and form these into small piles on pieces of clean paper towel.
3. Think of elegant patterns and carefully sketch these designs in light pencil on the eggshells. Consider the color, texture, and shape of the herbs in your design.

(continued on next page)

4. Use glue to attach the various parts of the herbs to the eggs so as to replicate the patterns you have drawn.

5. *Optional*: If you feel ambitious, use some ⅛-inch wooden dowels, colored yarn, and your finished Easter eggs to create a colorful Easter egg mobile (see illustration). Use one dowel as the top piece, then attach another dowel to each end of that to form a second tier. Adjust the point of attachment for each dowel so that the weight is balanced. You will hang 7 eggs in all.

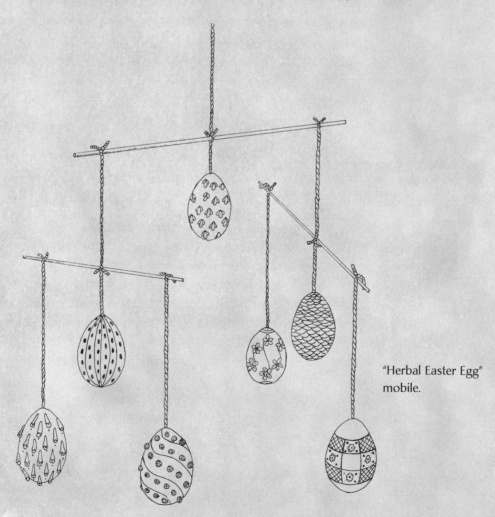

"Herbal Easter Egg" mobile.

6. For each egg: Tie a length of yarn onto a ½-inch-long piece of toothpick. Slip the toothpick into the hole on top of the egg and let it fall inside. Pull gently on the exposed end of the yarn and the toothpick with catch inside the egg.
7. Slide the points of attachment for each egg along the dowels until everything balances.

Herbal Easter Basket

MATERIALS:

Clean and dry flower petals or leaves of herbs
Glue or needle and thread
Sweetgrass or sprigs of lavender and rosemary

1. Instead of using store-bought plastic Easter grass or wood shavings, fill Easter baskets with a bed of rose petals and other dried herbs with sweet and floral aromas.
2. Glue or sew sweetgrass or sprigs of lavender and rosemary onto the handle and around the edge of the basket to add a touch of scent to the sweets within.

Herbal Christmas Decorations

MATERIALS:

Paper bag

Scissors

2-foot-square off-white or light blue cotton cloth

Common pins

Pencil

Sewing shears

*Needle and thread to match or complement the color
  of the cloth*

Dried violet flowers

Cloves

Crushed cinnamon sticks

Other herbs of your choice

1. Trace the simple outline of a dove, crescent moon, or other pleasing shape onto the paper bag to form a template.
2. Fold the cloth so that the "right" side faces out and pin it to the template.
3. Use sewing shears to cut out the shape, but be sure to leave an extra ¼ inch on the outside of the pencil line so there will be an extra margin of cloth to hem.
4. Remove the template and neatly sew the two pieces together almost all the way around, but leave the bottom open.
5. Fill the ornament with dried violet flowers, cloves, crushed cinnamon sticks, and other herbs of your choice, and then hand sew the bottom seam closed.
6. Attach a loop of thread along the top of the ornament in a spot where its weight will balance when hung. Think of other herbal cloth decorations to make, such as bells, balls, small dolls, and so on.

Herbal Christmas Tree Centerpiece

MATERIALS:

Ice pick, nut pick, or skewer
One 9-inch-high green Styrofoam cone
Scissors
Pruning clippers
Dried herbs of your choice.

1. Use an ice pick, nut pick, or skewer to push holes that are about 1 inch deep, ½ -inch apart, and angled down slightly into the Styrofoam cone.
2. Trim the stems of the dried herbs to about 3 inches long near the bottom of the tree and grading to 1 inch long near the top. Poke one stem into each hole on the outside of the cone, being careful to consider color and texture of herbs to create a pleasing arrangement.

Herbs on a Cone

MATERIALS:

Glue
Leaves, flowers, and seeds of herbs of your choice
Pinecone
Scissors
6-inch piece of yarn

1. Glue colorful and aromatic herbal leaves, flowers, and seeds onto the scales of a small pinecone, trimming as needed.
2. Attach a piece of yarn and hang on the Christmas tree.

Hanukkah Candles

MATERIALS:

9 herbal candles (see materials and directions provided for the chapter 2 activity "A Light of Life" on page 51)

Herbs or herbal oils of your choice: ginger, bay, borage, thyme, clove, patchouli, or frankincense

Hanukkah menorah

1. Make 9 herbal candles—one for each holder in the Hanukkah menorah.
2. Use herbs that promote courage, kindness, and faith. Ginger, bay, borage, and thyme impart courage and strength. Essence of clove protects and inspires courage. Patchouli invigorates and raises the spirits. Oil of frankincense helps strengthen and renew faith and brings life into balance.

Valentine's Day Heart for the Heart

MATERIALS:

Paper bag

2-foot-square red cotton cloth

Common pins

Pencil

Sewing shears

Needle and red thread

1 cup dried rose petals

Several drops rose oil

Small bowl

Spoon

1. Use the initial procedure described under "Herbal Christmas Decorations" on page 71, only design the template to create red cloth hearts and sew the two halves of the cloth heart together so the material is inside out. Leave a 3-inch space unsewn along one side of the heart, then turn it right-side out.
2. Stir the rose petals and several drops of rose oil together in a bowl, and let the mix sit for about 30 minutes so the oil can thoroughly soak into the flower petals.
3. Fill each heart with the rose petals and sew the final seam closed.

Valentine's Day Card

MATERIALS:

Piece of 8½- x 11-inch red posterboard

Scissors

Pencil

Clear glue

Rose petals

Colored pencils

One 5- x 6-inch envelope

1. Cut the piece of red posterboard in half to create two pieces that measure 8½ inches long by 5½ inches wide. Fold each piece in half to create a greeting card.
2. Trace a heart on the front of the card and glue rose petals into the shape of that heart.
3. Use colored pencils to write your own, personal message to your "Valentine" on the inside of the card. Place in envelope and send to your Valentine.

Ramadan Beverage

MATERIALS:

> *¼ cup hibiscus flowers*
> *Half-gallon pitcher full of drinking water*
> *Strainer*
> *About 2 tablespoons date sugar or honey*
> *Long-handled spoon*

A traditional drink during Ramadan, the ninth month of the Muslim religious year, is made with hibiscus flowers. This drink is consumed during *Iftar* meals, which are prepared after sun-down during the days of fasting.

1. Place the hibiscus flowers into a pitcher filled with water and stir. Let this soak in a cool place for about a day.
2. Pour this liquid through a strainer to remove the flowers.
3. Sweeten by adding a touch of traditional date sugar or honey and stir well.

Pots of Herbs

MATERIALS:

6 herb seeds or seedlings of your choice
A small planting pot for each herb
Light potting soil
Waterproof tray
Watering can

1. Make a list of the 6 or so herbs that you use most often in your cooking, healing, and craft work.
2. Fill the same number of small pots with light potting soil and line these up in a long, waterproof tray.
3. Plant seeds or seedlings of each of your favorite herbs—one herb for each pot.
4. Place the pots indoors in a sunny window. Keep them watered as needed and soon you will have a fresh, handy supply of your favorite herbs.

Interfaith Manna from Heaven

MATERIALS:

Ingredients listed for charoset *recipe (see page 80)*

Herbs for salad that you choose for their flavors and virtues (see pages 80–81)

Romaine lettuce

Seder bread (matzah)

Sharing a meal is an ancient tradition for bringing diverse people together with the intent of building community. Eating a meal of unleavened bread is one way of seeking wisdom and opening oneself to the spirit of God. In the Jewish mystical tradition, the Zohar emphasizes the connection between manna and the Divine. Bread is food of the heart that nourishes kindness and love.

1. Here is a simple recipe for *charoset* to eat with the Seder bread. It is followed by a list of herbs and their associated virtues. Choose the herbs whose flavors appeal to you, and whose qualities you seek. Choose wisely and add small quantities of these herbs into a salad of romaine lettuce to accompany the Seder meal.

2. Organize an interfaith potluck meal to which everyone will bring a dish that is symbolic of his or her faith and beliefs.

3. Begin the potluck by offering this Seder bread to others in the form of a blessing, sharing the names of the salad herbs and the symbolic meaning of each. Share the meaning of the *charoset* and invite everyone to enjoy its sweet taste on their Seder bread. Note that cinnamon is said to put people in good spirits and that ginger symbolizes courage and love.

4. Then, in turn, invite people to introduce the dishes that they brought to share with others something about their faith and the symbolic spiritual meaning of their entrées.

(continued on next page)

5. Before the meal begins, encourage everyone to choose the dishes they want to eat based not only on the appealing aspects of taste, smell, and appearance but also with a mind for feeding the spirit. Ask people to eat their meals with the intent of nourishing both body and spirit. Encourage diners to share with others the spiritual reasons why they chose the particular foods to eat.

Traditional (Ashkenazi) Charoset

2 large apples, cored and finely chopped
½ cup walnuts or almonds, finely chopped
2 teaspoons cinnamon

½ teaspoon ginger
1 tablespoon honey
Kosher wine

1. Combine the chopped apples and nuts in a medium-sized bowl.
2. Measure the cinnamon, ginger, and honey into a small bowl and stir to an even consistency.
3. Spoon the mixture of spices and honey into the bowl containing chopped apples and nuts. Blend thoroughly.
4. Dribble small amounts of Kosher wine into the mixture and stir until the charoset takes on a thick, mortar-like consistency.
5. Refrigerate overnight.

Here are some herbs and associated virtues to choose from for including in potluck dishes for "Interfaith Manna from Heaven." Herbs with an asterisk (*) can also be incorporated into salads.

Basil*: love, good wishes
Bay: love
Cardamom: attracts love
Coriander: modesty
Dill*: love
Fennel*: strength
Garlic: life energy, purification
Ginger*: love, courage
Mint*: virtue, love, and passion
Parsley*: festivals and feasting, knowledge

Sage*: wisdom, long life
Thyme: affection, courage, and strength

ALTERNATIVE ACTIVITY: Create your own meals using herbs with special virtues to celebrate and honor other spiritual celebrations, holidays, and feasts.

COMPLEMENTARY ACTIVITY: Create some floral arrangements for the tables at your interfaith potluck using the activity "Cosmic Community Centerpieces" on page 128.

Ritual Cleansing for Meals

MATERIALS:

Large jar or pitcher of fresh water
Sprigs and branches of fresh hyssop

1. Hyssop is used widely for cleansing and purification. Fill a large jar or pitcher with fresh water.
2. Take fresh sprigs of hyssop and soak them in this water for a day or so to extract the scent and essence.
3. Use fresh hyssop branches to sprinkle this water over the tables as a blessing before a feast, around the space where a spiritual ceremony is to be held, or upon the heads of those who have gathered for a celebration.

Daily Havdalah Spice Box

MATERIALS:

Small ornate box
1 teaspoon each cloves, cinnamon sticks, and cardamom

1. Find a small, fancy box, such as the kind that jewelry comes in, or one of the ornately carved boxes found in arts and crafts stores.
2. Place some cloves, pieces of cinnamon sticks, and open cardamom pods into the spice box.
3. Keep this spice box in your purse, briefcase, or book bag during the week at work and school. Whenever you feel harried, overwhelmed, or simply stressed out, find a quiet place to relax, then open your spice box and let the scents waft over you as a reminder of the good feelings that come with engaging in your favorite pastimes during Shabbat or on other holy days.

Egyptian–Style Thanksgiving Garland

MATERIALS:

Palm fronds

Light twine

*Flowers of your choice: lotus, delphinium, larkspur, and
  red poppy*

This garland can be interwoven among the meals and center-pieces on tables that are set for religious feasts. Each garland represents an herbal offering of thanksgiving for the feast. The flowers listed above were used as offerings in traditional Egyptian garlands.

1. Separate the palm fronds into long fibers.
2. Lay 9 fibers next to each other, tie the ends together, and hang the end on a hook.
3. Gather the fibers into 3 groups of 3 fibers each and braid them.
4. After you do the braiding, incorporate the stems of flowers of your choice into the skein.
5. Tie off the other end of the braid when it is completed.

Alternative procedure:

1. Complete step 1 as described above.
2. Gather the fibers into three groups of 3 fibers each and form each set into a cord by twisting to the right. As you work down the skein, the twisted cords will naturally wrap together to the left to form a rope garland.
3. When you reach the end, tie all of the fibers together.
4. Slip flower stems into the rope by twisting it slightly to create spaces as you move along its length.

Pots of Potpourri

MATERIALS:

1 quart dried herbs from among those listed below
Medium-sized bowl
Spoon
Powdered spices (cinnamon, clove, and ginger)
1 teaspoon essential oil (rose, clove, eucalyptus, or citron)
Fragrant water (rose, orange, or hyssop)
Small potpourri pots

Set potpourri out on the table whenever you are celebrating a holiday meal. Use herbs, spices, essential oils, and fragrant waters that are meant to whet the appetite, enliven the celebration, and enhance a joyous occasion.

1. Obtain about 1 quart (total) of dried flowers, leaves, fruit, and bark from among the herbs you choose for making potpourri: rose petals, bay leaves, lavender flowers and leaves, violet petals, rosemary, star anise, cloves, cinnamon, jasmine flowers, orange peel, and blue cornflowers.
2. In a medium-sized bowl, mix these herbs with two or three dashes of powdered spices, such as cinnamon, clove, and ginger. Mix these dry ingredients thoroughly.
3. Now sprinkle in 1 teaspoon of essential oil, such as rose, clove, eucalyptus, or citron. Moisten this with rosewater, orange water or the purifying hyssop water described under "Ritual Cleansing for Meals" on page 82.
4. Put portions of this potpourri into small, attractive pots, placing one pot on every table.

Herbs and Flowers for
Circle of Life

Anise
Balsam
Basil, sweet,
  purple (opal),
  lemon
Betony
Camelia
Caraway
Cardamom
Catmint
Cedar
Celandine
Chamomile
Chicory
Cinnamon
Clematis
Clove
Clover, red
  and white
Cornflower
Cumin

Daisy, oxeye
Dandelion
Eucalyptus
Fenugreek
Frankincense
Ginger
Ginseng
Hollyhock
Hyacinth
Hyssop
Jasmine
Joe-Pye weed
Lamb's quar-
  ters
Lavender
Lily
Lotus
Lupine
Mandrake
Marigold
Marjoram

Mint
Musk
Myrrh
Myrtle
Olive
Orange
Peppermint
Poppy
Rose, red
  (flowers and
  hips)
Rosemary
Rue
Saffron crocus
Sage
Snapdragon
Spearmint
Thyme
Violet
Wormwood

4

CIRCLE OF LIFE

It is the beautiful flower
that lends its scent to those herbs,
all that had shriveled and wilted.
It brings them lush greenness once more.
—Hildegard of Bingen

In the full leaf of late summer, when I walk through our herb garden, I often circle it sunwise, moving in the direction in which our home star arches across the sky. In the garden's center, which represents the nexus of the cosmos, stand the erect stems of the lofty Joe-Pye weed, whose flowers are so tall I must look up at them. This beloved herb is named after a famous Mohican healer, who once used it to cure a variety of ailments, including kidney stones and typhus. When I stoop down to pick and taste some leaves from our three beds of basil growing nearby, I say "Thank you" for the gift of the anise-like taste of the sweet variety, the complex aroma of opal basil, or the touch of citric flavor of my favorite, lemon basil.

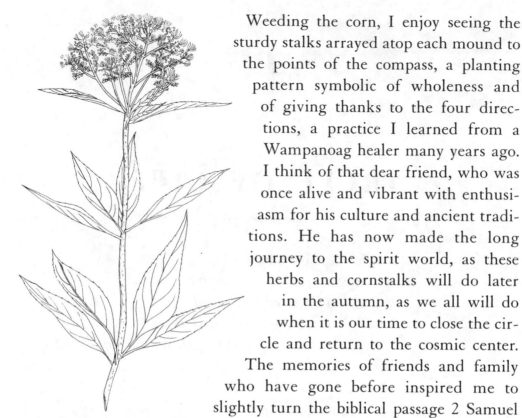

Joe-Pye weed or "queen of the meadow," a Native American healing herb.

Weeding the corn, I enjoy seeing the sturdy stalks arrayed atop each mound to the points of the compass, a planting pattern symbolic of wholeness and of giving thanks to the four directions, a practice I learned from a Wampanoag healer many years ago. I think of that dear friend, who was once alive and vibrant with enthusiasm for his culture and ancient traditions. He has now made the long journey to the spirit world, as these herbs and cornstalks will do later in the autumn, as we all will do when it is our time to close the circle and return to the cosmic center. The memories of friends and family who have gone before inspired me to slightly turn the biblical passage 2 Samuel 12:23 and hold it up to reflect their light:

It is a small consolation to know,
that one day we will go to join them.
But our hearts ache with the truth—
that they can no longer come to see us.

LIFE AND DEATH

There is a peace that comes from being so close to the garden's symbolic center of the cosmos, so alive with a palpable sense that here the circle of life and death turns each day as freely as bees gather nectar for the hive. It is no wonder that traditional Islamic gardens, especially those in Persia and Muslim India, have long been the final resting place for those who lovingly watered the roots and tended the seeds and shoots of their green brothers and sisters. There they began the long journey between earth and heaven. Perhaps this juxtaposition of cosmic realms inspired two Islamic words for garden, *firdaus* and *rauda*, which mean, respectively, "paradise" and "mausoleum."

Frankincense and myrrh have long been burned in the Arab world to create sacred smoke that rises as a bridge between the spirits of this world and the heavens. Jews and Muslims have burned frankincense as a funeral offering. Oil of frankincense was used in ancient Egypt to anoint the head of someone who had died. Myrrh—whose name comes for the Arabic *murr*, or "bitter"—first appeared in Exodus 30:23. To the ancient Hebrews, myrrh represented the pain and suffering of loss and was once used to anoint the dead.

Herbs have also been used to preserve the bodies of the deceased. Cinnamon and myrrh were often employed to embalm Egyptian mummies, attesting to the long-term ability of these herbs to inhibit the growth of bacteria and fungi. Rosemary was also used. Corpses were sometimes covered with an inch-deep layer of these herbs.

Ritual cleansing with lustral water after the death of a loved one is an ancient tradition. "Then one who is ritually clean shall take hyssop and dip it in the water. He must then sprinkle the tent, all the vessels and everyone there" (Numbers 19:18). Myrrh has often been used to purify the dead. Jesus was offered myrrh and wine while he was dying on the cross, and his body was rubbed with myrrh before he was laid to rest. Early Christians commonly buried the dead with spices and oils. Cedar wood has also been used for purification (Leviticus 14:4).

GRIEF AND RENEWAL

One reason that so many of us live our daily lives feeling emotionally wounded is that the contemporary way of life does not allow us time to properly resolve our grief. From the Italian family I was raised in to a number of Native American cultures I have come to know, the traditional period of mourning after losing a beloved was at least one year.

Nowadays, we are given a day or two off from work, then we're expected to put grief behind us, to "move on." But as we resume our daily routine, we are aware of a dull pain, an elegiac veil over our heart that can become a constant companion if we do not allow ourselves the time, energy, and space to pass through the stages of loss.

Even in laughter the heart finds sadness, and joy makes way for sorrow.

—Proverbs 14:13

For a time, we are suspended between these two poles of human experience. Then, after our grief, there comes a renewal. When the child of King David and Uriah's wife was taken gravely ill, he appealed to God in prayer and by fasting and sleeping on the ground under a piece of sack cloth. After the child died, David washed, anointed himself with oil, and dressed in clean clothes (2 Samuel 12:16–20).

LOVE AND CONNECTION

As the great circle turns, our sorrows transform into joy. The days and nights of loss start to lose their hold on us. Once again we notice the sweet songs of birds, the scents and colors of herbs and flowers, the beauty of a butterfly's wing. The face of a child sends rays of light into our heart. A loved one takes our hand and we feel the warmth and spark of old. The power of connection, the essence of life, beckons, and we rejoin the dance of the living.

Although *love* may grow in our hearts, the seeds of attraction are planted in our senses. Herbs are the essence of union—their elixir is the catalyst of the cosmic connection that we call a *wedding*. Egyptians created lavish arrangements of herbs and flowers to celebrate weddings and feasts, including sprigs and flowers from basil and sage, chicory, myrtle, chamomile, wormwood, and olive. Lotus bread was served, made from the flower of life. Women who lived in the time of the pharaohs attracted men by wearing "unguent cones" on their heads. These tall, dome-shaped caps were a blend of animal fat scented with herbs. As the fat melted, its essence was infused into hair and clothing. With one kiss, beauty got into the eyes of the beholder.

Perfume comes from Old Italian, *parfumo*, "to fill with smoke." Vapors from the saffron crocus open our hearts with mirth and stimulate the appetites. Essence of rosewater and the scent of basil imbue the heart with ethereal love. In the sixteenth century, Hindu brides wore their hair plaited and interwoven with sprigs and flowers of hyacinth. All of these essences paled next to the powerfully magnetic scent of musk, the "herb of love."

Frankincense and myrrh have been used for perfume for five thousand years, and have long been offered to sanctify a marriage. Myrrh's name may reflect its bitter taste, but its soft scent projects a hint of anise, and it is the archetypal perfume of the ancients. Esther may have won the heart of King Ahasuerus, but not before bathing "... six months with oil of myrrh, and six months with spices and lotions commonly used for feminine beauty treatment" (Esther 2:12–13). Myrrh and frankincense still comprise the grounding essence in many of today's popular perfumes, including Le Jardin, Alliage, Opium, and Eau de Caron (myrrh), and Soir de Paris, Replique, Jicky, and Youth Dew (frankincense).

> *Who is this approaching*
> *up from the desert,*
> *in columns of smoke,*
> *fragrant with myrrh and frankincense,*
> *rare spices and herbs*
> *of the wandering merchants?*
>
> —Song of Songs 3:6

THE WEDDING JOURNEY

Herbals are also used symbolically at weddings. Garlands of marjoram are woven into small wreaths and worn atop the heads of both brides and grooms in Greece to symbolize the unbroken circle of their union. In Victorian England, beauty and excellence were expressed in bouquets festooned with blossoms of camellia, while caraway inspired newlyweds to remain faithful. And the *mustaceum*, a traditional Roman wedding cake, was flavored with anise and cumin.

Some years ago, after our own wedding, my wife, Marie, and I honeymooned in Italy, where we stayed with my relations in Pietravairano, a small village situated about one hundred miles south and east of Rome. On the first day, the seven of us piled into a small European sedan and raced north along the highway en route to visit the *Abbazia de Montecassino*, the ancient monastic birthplace of the Benedictine order, which sits atop a steep-sided mountain that rises dramatically from the plains of Frosinone. Although the original cathedral had been leveled by bombs during World War II, its reincarnation was now nearing completion. The ornate altar was adorned with intricate designs formed by inlays of lapis lazuli, as pure as an azure sky. Many of the panels on the restored dome overhead had been repainted by hand, each separated by a line of sculpted plaster that appeared as the frosting on a birthday cake. The spicy essences of frankincense and myrrh hung in the air, evoking memories of countless Sunday blessings during the preparation of communion.

We spent much of our second day touring King Ferdinand's palace and walking in the expansive gardens of Caserta. This magnificent palace was originally built in the middle of the eighteenth century by the Bourbon King Charles III, expressly to rival the exquisite architecture and grand setting of Versailles. Our small family group made the best of this breathtaking site. As the sun arched higher and the light of midday colored the gardens with its brush of flat, pastel light, we sat along the wall of one of the many pools and ate our lunch of hazelnut ice cream, *gelato nocciola*. Licking this delectable treat in the sweltering heat, my mind wandered. I thought of the many ways that European herbal lore connected hazelnuts to steps along the circle of life: foretelling a woman's fate in marriage; predicting the number and the gender of children a couple would bear; presaging whether an ill-stricken person would survive.

Then we walked the grand, two-mile-long series of pools and fountains and visited the English garden, where we found a naturalized

landscape replete with familiar herbs
and flowers. At first, it seemed odd
to me that I should know so
many plants—oxeye daisy,
Queen Anne's lace, chamomile,
red and white clover, lamb's quarter, celandine, and the like. Then I
recalled that, like my own family,
these plants were native to Europe
and had been introduced to
North America in relatively
recent times. Both herbs
and ancestors had taken
root in a new land.

When we finally
approached the far end of
the procession of fountains,
the sun had bleached our energy
and spirits. There we found a colos-
sal fountain in which a magnificent
statue of Diana (Artemis), the Roman
goddess of the hunt, was bathing with her
maidens. Nearby, the unfortunate hunter
Actaeon had happened upon them, only to

Plants from Europe have naturalized in
North America (left to right): celandine,
oxeye daisy, Queen Anne's lace, and red
clover.

be transformed by Diana into a stag for his transgression. In this dra-
matic depiction of the story, Actaeon's own pack of hounds is poised,
ready to devour him. Step by labored step, we climbed the series of
fountains until we reached the source stream, where it emerged after a
long journey, having been diverted by a viaduct from distant mountain
waters, twenty-six miles away.

That evening, when we returned to my relative's home in
Pietravairano and entered our bedroom to rest and refresh in anticipation of the elaborate dinner that was to come, we discovered that a

life-sized baby doll had been placed in the center of our bed. The placement of this *bambino*, we were told, was a blessing offered to visiting newlyweds, in hope that there would be many children in the years to come, to continue the circle of life.

> Good people,
> most royal greening verdancy,
> rooted in the sun,
> you shine with radiant light.
> In this circle of earthy existence
> you shine so finely,
> it surpasses understanding.
> God hugs you.
> You are encircled by the arms
> of the mystery of God.
>
> —Hildegard of Bingen

Myrrh and frankincense, I would later learn, are also a part of the renewal of life, of opening the circle to a new being. Frankincense is burned as a traditional blessing for a mother and her newborn child; the baby is anointed with oil and enveloped in the sacred smoke. This, and all the herbs that are gifts from God, are the root of our connection to all of creation, be it life that flows with blood of red, or green.

These herbs were offered as a gift to honor a most sacred birth, to welcome a holy one into this world. "The sight of the star filled them with delight, and going into the house they saw the child with his mother, Mary, and falling to their knees they did him homage. Then, opening their treasures, they offered him gifts of gold and frankincense and myrrh" (Matthew 2:10–12).

Herbal Memorial: Lustral Water

MATERIALS:

Fresh sprigs of hyssop
Large glass bottle of water
Small ornate vessel with cap

Blessing with hyssop is an ancient tradition after the passing of a loved one. Hyssop cleanses the spirit and sanctifies whomever and whatever it touches. Preparing and using lustral water is a way to honor the loss of someone you love.

1. Soak sprigs of hyssop in a glass bottle full of water for several days.
2. Pour this water into a small, ornate vessel, cap it off, and take it with you to the burial service. Bring a fresh sprig of hyssop as well.
3. During the burial service, when there is an opportunity for those present to share, say your words of remembrance and blessing, then sprinkle the earth, urn, or casket with the lustral water.

Herbal Memorial:
Egyptian Floral Bouquet

MATERIALS:

Fresh flowers that you choose from those listed below

Pruning clippers

Yarn

Moist paper towel

Plastic wrap

Brightly colored wrapping that measures 12 x 6 inches
(paper, piece of felt cloth, etc.)

Scissors

Ribbon

Flowers and herbs are often presented at memorial services and at times of celebrating the life of one whose spirit has moved on. But what do those flowers mean, and what could bring even deeper meaning to that gift? Ancient Egyptians presented bouquets as a gift to friends and loved ones to symbolize protection, long life, or the memory of someone dear. Bouquets were also set out as adornments for wedding ceremonies, celebrations, and memorials.

1. In addition to various grasses, rushes, palms, and long branches of olive, here are some traditional Egyptian herbs and flowers: lotus, poppy, cornflower, hollyhock, snapdragon, clematis, lavender, lupine, and lily. Cut to equal length the stems of some of these herbs and flowers, or others you have chosen.
2. Use yarn to tie the ends together to form a pleasing arrangement.
3. Moisten a piece of paper towel well and wrap it around the ends of the stems. Enclose the paper towel in a piece of plastic wrap to keep the flowers fresh.

4. Now take some beautiful, brightly colored paper, felt cloth, or other attractive natural wrapping and cut a strip that is about 12 inches long x 6 inches wide. Wrap this around the base of the bouquet to create a 6-inch collar.
5. Tie this collar on with yarn and finish off with an attractive ribbon of a complementary color.

Bereavement Bouquet

MATERIALS:

Dried herbs of your choice that are still on the stems (rose, rue, eucalyptus, betony, and rosemary)

Pruning clippers

Yarn

Brightly colored wrapping that measures 12 x 6 inches (paper, piece of felt cloth, or the like)

Scissors

Ribbon

Vase

Photograph or other memento of the person you wish to remember

1. Here are some herbs that can be included in a bereavement bouquet to help you honor and heal your relationship with the deceased: rose and rue (forgiveness), eucalyptus (spiritual healing), betony (healing of the whole person), and rosemary (remembrance and revitalization of love for that person).

2. Use these herbs to create an arrangement as described in the previous activity, "Egyptian Floral Bouquet." In this case, however, the stems of dried herbs only need to be tied together with yarn, without the moist wrapping and water.

3. Wrap the bouquet in paper and tie with ribbon. Put this bouquet in a dry vase and keep it in a special place in your living space to honor the loved one you have lost. If you like, keep a favorite photograph of your loved one by the bouquet. Whenever you miss your loved one, or have something you want to share or say, go to that place and speak to her or him, or simply visit in silence and listen for that person's voice.

4. As time passes, you many find a desire for a symbolic "letting go" of your grief. Take the bereavement bouquet to one of your loved one's favorite places, such as a beach, river, park, or mountaintop. Say one last good-bye and place the bouquet on that spot, or toss it into the water. Now comes the time to focus on your own renewal, on what lies ahead.

Egyptian Herbal Oil

Materials:

1 pint high-quality olive oil

Wide-mouthed glass jar

1 teaspoon each of ground cinnamon, thyme, and cardamom

Cheesecloth

Attractive long-necked bottle

Cinnamon sticks

Crushed leaves of myrtle

1. Here is an oil that is easy to prepare. It contains herbs to express your love and affection. Pour a pint of quality olive oil into a wide-mouth glass jar.
2. Add 1 teaspoon each of ground cinnamon (love and desire), thyme (affection), cardamom (draws in love), and crushed myrtle leaves (beauty, passion, and love). Stir well.
3. Allow this to sit at room temperature for as long as two weeks but at lease a few days.
4. Pour through several layers of cheesecloth to strain out the remains of herbs.
5. Find a fancy, long-necked bottle and drop a few cinnamon sticks into the neck, then pour the prepared oil into this bottle.
6. The best way to present this oil as a gift to someone you love is to offer a massage, but only if you're ready to offer the peace imparted by the olive oil, combined with the powers of love and attraction instilled by the other herbs.

Marriage Blessing: Marjoram Marriage Garlands

Sometimes, the most meaningful gifts are simple herbals that you make yourself. Following are two traditional herbal blessings you can bestow on a couple's wedding day.

MATERIALS:

> Long sprigs of marjoram
> Yarn

1. Weave or braid two simple head wreaths from long sprigs of marjoram, one for each partner.
2. Tie the ends together with colorful yarn. These elegant garlands are a traditional Greek blessing for peace, joy, and happiness in the couple's life together.

Marriage Blessing: Flower Blessing Rings

MATERIALS:

Fresh dandelion flowers attached to their stems

1. This is the perfect activity to do with children on the day of a wedding. Find a patch of dandelions or some marigold flowers and create chains of about 12 inches long. This is done by carefully parting the stem along its length, just below each blossom, then slipping the end of the next stem through that slit, and so on. Create chains of about 12 inches long, then gently use a long, supple stem to tie the ends together and form a ring.

2. These flower rings can be placed as blessings around or under anything that the wedding couple will use that day, such as wineglasses, plates, gifts, or even the wedding rings themselves.

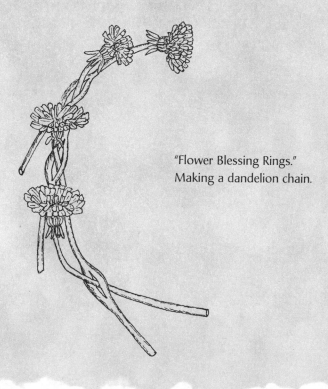

"Flower Blessing Rings."
Making a dandelion chain.

Egyptian Wedding Bouquet

MATERIALS:

Basil and other herbs that you choose for love, longevity, and attraction

Other materials listed under "Egyptian Floral Bouquet"

1. Incorporate herbs from the list of "Herbs for the Wedded" on pages 106–107 into an Egyptian Floral Bouquet, which is described on page 96. Make this a bouquet of flowers for love, longevity, and attraction. Sweet (green) basil was used in Egypt, and violet symbolized steadfast, loyal love.

Tea for Two

MATERIALS:

Tea bags from among the herbs listed below
Large urn for heating hot water
Cups
Spoons

1. Serve some teas during a wedding reception that are brewed from the list of "Herbs for the Wedded" on pages 106–107. Choose herbs that offer virtues for the wedded couple, and all those couples present, and that are easily found in prepared herbal teas, such as cardamom, chamomile, cinnamon, clove, ginger, jasmine, mint, orange, peppermint, rose, rose hips, and spearmint.

Promise of Pomanders

MATERIALS:

Oranges
Ice pick, nut pick, awl, or skewer
Whole cloves
Ground cinnamon
Bowl
Ribbon

1. Find some large, nicely shaped oranges. Take an ice pick, nut pick, awl, or other pointed object, clean it well, and use it to poke holes that are spaced ¼ inch apart in the skin of the fruit. You can also create patterns of holes in the shapes of hearts and other images that will mean something personal to the wedding couple.
2. Now stick cloves into the holes in the orange skin.
3. Put some ground cinnamon in a bowl and role the cloven pomanders in the cinnamon.
4. Dust off each orange, wrap a ribbon around it and tie a bow. Leave a long piece of ribbon sticking out for hanging.
5. Each element of these pomanders bears a symbolic meaning for the married couple: orange is for love and abundance; clove is for attraction; and cinnamon is for love, attraction, and good fortune.

Herbal Newlywed Blessings

MATERIALS:

Seeds

Flower petals, or leaves of herbs chosen from among those listed below

Small pouch to carry the plants in

More herbs seem to be associated with love, marriage, attraction, and fertility than anything else. Myrtle, violet, and rose are all regarded as the herbs of Venus—Roman goddess of love, beauty, and passion. Violet is associated with her Greek counterpart, Aphrodite. Mandrake is an archetypal herb of attraction whose name comes from the Hebrew word that means "to love." In the Book of Genesis, Jacob's wife, Leah, trades some mandrakes with his other wife and true love, Rachel, in exchange for the promise of a night with Jacob (Genesis 30:14–24). During an ancient Egyptian courtship rite, a man would cut a piece of mandrake while facing to the west, then dance around the herb while intoning words of love for the woman of his desire.

1. The timeworn tradition of throwing rice at the bride and groom after the wedding ceremony can be enriched by tossing the seeds, leaves, or flower petals from any of the herbs on the following list. This is a way of blessing a marriage with the chosen virtues given for each herb. But please use good judgment in choosing what to throw: rose petals raining down on a newly-wed couple will impart a fragrant wish for love, but no one wants to be pelted with bulbous rose hips when leaving the wedding ceremony.

HERBS FOR THE WEDDED

Bay: love, celebration
Camellia: beauty
Caraway: faithfulness
Cardamom: happiness, love, and health

Catnip: love

Chamomile: wishes come true

Clove: attraction

Clover: happy marriage, fertility

Dill: love

Jasmine: love

Lavender: sweet love, devotion, tranquility, peace, and good luck

Mandrake: fertility, love

Marjoram: joy, happiness, and peace

Mint: love, passion, and desire

Myrtle: beauty, passion, and love

Orange (small pieces of dried peel): love

Peppermint: warm feelings

Rose: love, beauty, and womanhood

Rosebud: purity, young beauty

Rosemary: tenderness, fidelity, beauty and remembrance

Sage: longevity, virtues of domesticity, and wisdom

Sorrel: affection

Spearmint: kindness, warm feelings

Vervain: intimacy, secrets, and confidences

Violet: steadfast love, loyalty, modesty, and happiness

Baby Blessings and Milk Biscuits

Long after the wedding night, anise, cumin, fennel, and fenugreek may be needed to help promote a mother's milk. Fenugreek is reputed to aid in delivery at birth. (**Check with a medical professional before using any herbs while pregnant or nursing.**) Oils of myrrh and frankincense are used to anoint the foreheads of mother and child as a blessing. Meanwhile, here is one *sweet* recipe for helping to bless a new mother and her baby.

Milk (Anise) Biscuits (Biscotti Anisette)

YIELD: about 10 dozen biscuits

DOUGH

1 cup sugar	5 cups flour
1 cup oil	3 tablespoons baking powder
1 cup milk	1-pound box powdered sugar
3 eggs, beaten	4 tablespoons warm milk (add more as needed)
3 teaspoons lemon extract	1 teaspoon vanilla extract
3 or 4 drops anise extract	Colored sprinkles

1. Preheat oven to 350°F.
2. Blend the sugar, oil, milk, beaten eggs, and lemon and anise extracts until smooth.
3. Mix the flour and baking powder, then combine with the wet ingredients and blend well. The dough should be dry enough to be worked with your hands. Add a bit more flour if it is sticky.
4. Roll the dough into 1-inch balls and place 2 inches apart on a greased cookie sheet. Bake for 8 to 10 minutes, until the underside, not the top, is golden brown.
5. Prepare the glaze while the biscuits are cooling. Mix the powdered sugar with about 4 tablespoons of warm milk and 1

teaspoon of vanilla extract. If necessary, carefully add small amounts of milk until the glaze is just a little thin.

6. Frost the biscuits when they have cooled but are still slightly warm to the touch. Use your fingertip and carefully coat the top of each biscuit with a dollop of frosting. You may want to drop some colored sprinkles onto the glazing while it is still wet. I prefer the smooth glaze on these tasty morsels, which seem to melt in your mouth.

Cosmic Herbs

Flowers, and Fruits

Almond
Balsam
Basil, sweet, purple (opal)
Bergamot (bee balm)
Betony
Borage
Butterwort
Calendula
Caraway
Cassia, pink
Cedar
Chamomile
Clover
Corn
Dandelion
Dill
Fennel
Frankincense
Galbanum

Garlic
Ginseng
Grape
Henna
Hyssop
Jasmine, white and yellow
Lavender
Lily, white and Madonna
Lotus
Marigold
Marjoram
Milkwort
Mint
Mustard tree
Myrrh
Myrtle
Narcissus
Nutgrass

Onycha
Parsley
Pepper, black
Pomegranate
Rose, red
Rosemary
Rowen (tree)
Rue, garden
Saffron crocus
Sage
Sandalwood
Savory, summer
Thyme
Turmeric
Verbena
Vervain
Violet
Willow
Wormwood
Yarrow

5

COSMIC HERBALS

Divinity is,
in its omniscience and omnipotence,
like a wheel,
a circle,
a whole,
that can neither be understood,
nor divided,
nor begun, nor ended.
Just as a circle embraces all
that is within it,
so does the Godhead embrace all.

—Hildegard of Bingen

On the third day, God created herbs (Genesis 1:11–12). In the east, God planted a garden, a paradise for the first people. There, in the center of paradise, God planted the Tree of Life, whose branches bore the knowledge of good and evil. From the base of this tree arose a river that divided into four streams that reached out across the land (Genesis 2:8–10).

This image is a fundamental archetype of creation. The paradigm of the cosmos as being a circle composed of the four quarters of the universe is found throughout the world's spiritual traditions, including Christianity, Judaism, Islam, Hinduism, and the beliefs of numerous indigenous peoples. The center of this circle often represents the intersection between heaven and earth, the balance point of the cosmos. This is a place where we can go for spiritual renewal and awareness, a nexus between our lives and the Divine.

THE ELEMENTAL COSMOS

Hildegard of Bingen's paintings portray the universe as a sphere divided equally into the four realms of water, air, earth, and fire. These four elements are the source of humankind's wisdom and our creative energy, our *viriditas*, or "greening power." Together, they represent the world in balance. In one of Hildegard's paintings, which depicts the renewal of heaven and earth, the ring of creation encompasses flowers, water, and herbs, as well as the stars in the sky.

> No one has the power
> to divide this circle,
> to surpass it,
> or to limit it.
> —*Hildegard of Bingen*

How do we reconcile this paradox of the cosmic circle, which is at once whole and indivisible, and yet composed of constituent parts, each of which helps us grow as we seek the Divine through the full realization of our own creative spirit? Perhaps the answer rests in the heart of the circle, where the first tree rooted and bore the fruit of wisdom, where the first herbs unfurled their leaves and opened their petals to a new day, rich with the promise of completion.

The blowing wind, the mild moist air,
the exquisite greening of trees and grasses—
In their beginning, in their ending,
they give God their praise.

—Hildegard of Bingen

In these cosmologies, herbs arose from the center of the nascent universe bearing gifts for the spirit. Ginseng is one source of food and medicine believed to have come down from heaven to help us here on Earth. Ancient Egyptians associated each of the four elements with particular herbs: galbanum (earth), myrrh (water), onycha (air), and frankincense (fire) A secret blend of herbs known as *Kyphi*, which could only be prepared by the religious, was burned to form a pathway on which spirits could journey to heaven.

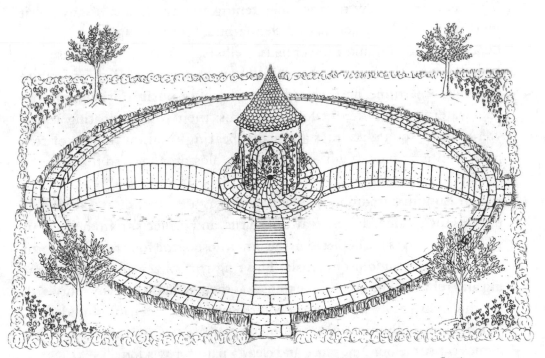

Ancient Islamic gardens were designed as circles divided into quarters, reflecting a vision of the cosmos found among spiritual traditions around the world.

Ancient Islamic gardens were living metaphors for paradise and were designed with a most pleasing array of patterns, textures, heights, colors, and scents. In one traditional design, four stone footbridges arched out from the center toward the four directions. At the intersection of the bridges stood a vine-covered pavilion with a pointed roof, whose pillars were intertwined with grape. Each garden symbolized the nexus of heaven and earth. Worshippers crossed these bridges to reach the center of a circular pool of water.

Among the Arab gardens of Spain grew many familiar herbs, including marjoram, chamomile, lavender, myrtle, thyme, saffron, mint, and basil. In season, branches of pomegranate, almond, and pink cassia trees hung pendulous with fruit. Indian frankincense (agar) and sandalwood

A garden is a mirror of a mind.

—Henry Beston, *Herbs and the Earth*

(chandan) trees grew nearby, heightening the awareness of any spirit who strolled the garden paths. Henna buds unfurled to form delicate petals of white or pink. Flower beds, trellises, and hanging baskets were adorned with the aromatic blossoms of violet, narcissus, red rose, white and yellow jasmine, and white lily, a symbol of purity. Growing in the still waters were different forms of lotus; their round, floating leaves were fed by spoke-like rays and stalks bearing fragrant flowers of red, pink, white, or blue. Night-opening lotus blossoms showed their face to the stars and moon.

In Buddhist tradition, the lotus flower is a symbol of awakening. It purifies the garden, drives away evil spirits, and protects from their intrusion. Lotus leaves are depicted in the innermost of the four rings that form the edge of the Buddhist mandala. This ring symbolizes spiritual awakening and rebirth. The other three rings and their symbols, moving outward, are the eight graveyards (human consciousness and rebirth), thunderbolt or *vajra* circle (illumination), and the ring of fire (transformation), whose flames consume our ignorance and clear a path for wisdom.

Mandala is a word from Sanskrit that means, "circle" and "completion." It is the sacred Buddhist symbol of the universe. Each mandala is divided into four quarters that correlate with what are often called the "four boundless thoughts." These are loving-kindness, sympathy, compassion, and equanimity. In some traditions, the center is the heavens. The four directions—south, north, east, and west—are identified with air, water, earth, and fire. A square temple is set within the mandala, with its four gates facing these four aspects of the universe.

At the heart of this cosmic paradigm is a seed that is symbolically planted by the four Buddhist monks who create each new mandala of sand, each forming a quarter of the whole. Starting with the center, they work outward and in tandem so that the mandala image evolves as an interconnected whole. The mandala is a symbol—a place to go in the mind's eye during meditation. On the journey to our inner space, the images of the mandala come alive along the pathway to discovering life's precepts or guiding principles—the stepping stones to wisdom.

> *Yet, since you love sincerity of the heart, teach me the secrets of wisdom.*
>
> —Psalms 51:6

In one source of Buddhist wisdom, the Lotus Sutra's "parable of the herbs," all herbs are bathed in the same sunlight, watered by the same rain, and fed by the same soil, yet every herb is unique. The parts of each herb represent four progressive steps along our spiritual paths: roots (faith), stems (guiding principles), twigs (meditation), and leaves (wisdom). As spirits on this path, we come to possess and fully express our own virtues by growing our gifts and abilities.

Some sacred Buddhist gardens are enclosed. The center of the garden is the locus of the cosmos. Herbs are planted in this place where seekers come to contemplate and focus the mind. Healing herbs—black pepper, turmeric, and nutgrass—adorn the path to spiritual growth and enlightenment. As the fragrance of aromatic herbs and herbal blossoms waft over this space, the spirit is calmed, the body healed.

In the Hindu vision of the cosmos, Earth has four corners: sunrise, sunset, north, and south. Reflecting this sacred geography, the Hindu mandala forms another link in the quadrifid chain of cosmic conceptions. Growing at the center of creation is the plant that is considered most sacred among the Hindus: *Tulsi* or "Holy Basil." At the dawn of each day, the Hindu Vashnava pray first to basil, then to the Lord Krishna. In one morning prayer, holy water is poured into a vessel and carried reverently to a tree that grows in the center of the garden; the person circles the tree seven times before using the water to quench the thirst of Holy Basil. *Tulsi* symbolizes the goddess and wife of Vishnu, the preserver, for whom basil is woven into garlands and presented as an offering. Three of the Hindu spiritual observances that have incorporated the leaves of basil as part of the rituals are *tirth* (holy liquid), *prasad* (holy food), and *pooja* (worship of God).

Tulsi is a symbol of happiness, health, purity, and good fortune. Visitors to Hindu homes are offered a basin for washing the hands as well as bathwater in which basil flowers are floating. Basil is planted in home gardens, on the grounds of most temples, and under the stairs of churches, where it promotes harmony, lends protection, and helps open a pathway to heaven. Unmarried Hindu women pray to basil to help them find a husband who is kind and just. Wives pray for peace and prosperity at home. On special occasions, flowers are offered to the basil plants and a circle of lighted candles surrounds them.

> *Being is God's circle.*
> *And in this circle all creatures exist.*
> *Everything that is in God,*
> *is God.*
>
> —Meister Eckhart

Native to Africa and Asia, and known to the Greeks as *basilikon phuton*, "kingly herb," Holy Basil's Latin name is *Ocimum sanctorum*, "to smell sacred." Purple basil, whose leaves emanate a scent of clove, has its origins in India. The familiar green basil that bears white flowers comes from the Mediterranean. This beloved, aromatic plant is a symbol of peace, virtue, and piety toward God. In the courts of India, witnesses must often swear an oath of truth upon a sprig of Holy Basil.

The ancient healing practice of the Hindu faith, which is known as Ayurvedic medicine, employs minerals, herbs, and metals, including Kamlesh Ayurveda, aromatherapy. The healing virtues of basil are strengthened by mixing with another sacred plant, marjoram, as well as hyssop, lavender, and bergamot.

A cosmic image depicting the universe made whole by honoring the four aspects or directions is also found in many indigenous spiritual beliefs. In the traditions of the Abenaki culture of northeastern North America, this paradigm comes alive during the sweat lodge ceremony. After entering the yellow door of dawn in the East, *wôbanek*, one travels to the south, *nibenakik*, the place of things new and growing and green, and then to the west, the place of those things yet to come in the red of sunset, *nakihlôt*, which leads to life in the next world. One moves along the circle to the whiteness of the north, *pebonki*, the place of fasting, quiet, and clarity, of healing and peace.

SPIRIT GARDENS

In the seventh-century text of *De Genesi ad Litteram,* or *Literal Meaning of Genesis,* Saint Augustine wrote that paradise is a garden. In his teachings, he often referred to the parable of the mustard seed, saying Christ tended the garden and we are the fruit of that creation. "The kingdom of heaven is like a mustard seed which a man took and sowed in his field. It is the smallest of all the seeds, but when it has grown it is the biggest shrub of all and becomes a tree so that the birds of the air come and shelter in its branches" (Matthew 13:31–32; Mark 4:31–32). The mustard seed is a symbol of spiritual strength, growth, and resolve. "I tell you solemnly, if your faith were the size of a mustard seed you could say to this mountain, 'Move from here to there,' and it would move; nothing would be impossible for you" (Matthew 17:20–21).

By the twelfth and thirteenth centuries, during the time of Hildegard of Bingen and Meister Eckhart, medieval monastic gardens flourished. The writings of the Cistercians from this time reveal that they were passionate gardeners who believed that cultivating and growing herbs was one path to spiritual growth and devotion.

Symbolism sprouted and bloomed throughout the beds of the cloister garden. Borage was grown for courage and good cheer; fennel was cultivated as a source of strength and to encourage virtues worthy of praise. Chamomile was prized as a counterbalance that instilled a sense of humility. The Madonna lily personified the purity of the Virgin Mary. Christ's martyrdom was recalled in the blossoms of the red rose, and his blood flowed in the form of wine fermented from grapes plucked from overhanging arbors. Milk was sometimes blessed by weaving an herbal ring from flowers of the dandelion, marigold, milkwort, or butterwort, then placing the ring under the milk can while invoking the Father, Son, and Holy Spirit.

FOLKLORE AND MAGIC

Folklore occasionally penetrated the monastery garden. Tales from the Trie Cloister Garden in France tell of how only a virgin can catch a unicorn. If a captive unicorn is killed, it has the power to come back to life—a fantastical allegory for the death and resurrection of Jesus Christ.

Outside the high stone walls of the cloister, in the fertile soil of myth, the power of herbs inspired many tales. Some of the beliefs adapted over the centuries by Christians in Europe most likely grew out of ancient beliefs of the Druids and Celts. A five-leaf clover is unlucky—a portent of evil. The shamrock, or four-leaf clover, however, which is associated with Saint Patrick, is a good omen—a presage of "good luck." But don't try *searching* for a four-leaf clover, for they can only be found when one is not looking. An old Scottish blessing is made while resting the right hand on a sprig of yarrow. While signing to the four cardinal points of the cross, the well-wisher says, "In the name of the Father and Son and Spirit journey prosper."

Vervain is considered a sacred herb in the ancient traditions of many peoples, including the Greeks, Romans, and Druids. Greeks called it *Hierobotane*, "Holy Plant," and the Romans believed that brooms made from the purifying branches of this *Herba Sacra* were used to sweep clean the Jovian altars. Vervain was sacred among the Scandinavian priests who honored Thor and was believed to wield the powers of prophecy by the Magi—holy men and healers from ancient Persia and Media who sought wisdom among the stars and were students of nature.

Garden rue was thought to possess the power of magic. And it was said that the dark magic brought by the willow could be undone by wood of the rowan tree. Dill was associated with the mischievous Pan and summer savory with the Satyrs, woodland beings from Greek mythology who appeared as people with the legs, ears, and hooves of a goat. Even in medieval times—an age when religion and superstition were deeply intertwined—*Angelica archangelica* was known for its ability to ward off dark magic.

Savory would sit well in the center of the Buddhist mandala, since its seed is said to be of both this world and the spirit world. And that powerful connection, between these two realms of being, is central to our understanding of the relationship between herbs and the cosmos. Herbs were there at the beginning, at once reaching roots down into the fresh new earth

Flavorful dill has many spiritual associations, from protection against evil to a connection with the infamous Pan.

and arching limbs green with leaves toward the heavens. Whatever path we take on our spiritual journeys, herbs will grow along the way, patiently present, waiting to help us achieve a deeper understanding and oneness with the cosmos.

A Cosmic Herbal Garden

MATERIALS:

One tall stake

Scissors

String

Trowel

Compass

Birdbath or other garden centerpiece (optional)

Seeds and/or seedlings of the four complementary herbs you choose

Lime or fertilizer and other supplies needed to create optimal growing conditions for the herbs you plant

Waterproof marker

Wooden markers or Popsicle sticks to identify plants

Plant stakes

Watering can

Depending on the size of your garden, these standard gardening tools would be helpful: shovel, rake, hoe, pruning clippers, and work gloves

IF GROWING HERBS INDOORS: 1 large pot or 4 small pots, gravel (for bottom of each pot), and potting soil.

1. Create a simple herb garden designed after an essential image of the cosmos. Decide how large an area you want the garden to cover, then put a tall garden stake in the center. Cut a piece of string as long as the radius of the circle you want to create and tie it loosely around the stake. Walk the string around the stake while marking the edge of the circle in the soil with a trowel.

2. Using a compass, or the sun, divide the garden into four equal quadrants that are aligned with the four cardinal directions: north, south, east, and west. Mark pathways leading into the cosmic garden from each of the four directions. If space allows, create a place in the

(continued on next page)

center of the garden where you can sit and contemplate or meditate using some of the activities described in chapter 6. Since many visions of the cosmos include water in the center, you could incorporate a birdbath, sunken pool, or small fountain there.

3. If your garden area is limited, or if you live where there is no outdoor space to plant a garden, obtain a large pot and create a miniature cosmic garden in the home or on a patio or rooftop. You could also use four small pots aligned to the four directions.

4. Choose four different herbs discussed in this chapter to plant based on a symbolic theme for your garden, such as balance, spiritual enlightenment, healing, protection, spiritual connection with creation, purification, human virtues, or stages that you have passed through in your own life.

5. As you design the garden, be mindful of the virtues and qualities of each herb so that complementary herbs will be positioned in opposite quadrants to provide a sense of balance. Plant an herb that promotes courage and strength, for instance, diagonally across from one that imparts humility. A cosmic garden theme of love and connection could have this arrangement of herbs: mint for passion (north), lavender for peace (south), rose for love (east), and rosemary for fidelity (west). (See illustration on page 157.) A garden theme of spiritual growth virtues could include borage for courage (north), basil for protection (south), parsley for knowledge (east), and sage for wisdom (west).

Or you could create a sensory garden simply to celebrate the diversity of creation, choosing herbs for color, scent, texture, and taste. This cosmic garden could include herbs whose flowers attract hummingbirds and butterflies.

6. Obtain seeds or seedlings for the herbs you have chosen, then treat the soil with lime or fertilizer and plant them according to the needs of each particular plant. See chapter 7, "The Practical Realm," for ideas on obtaining, growing, and using herbs. Use the waterproof marker to write the names of the herbs on the small sticks, then push them into the ground where those herbs are planted.

7. Push stakes into the ground to support the plants, and then water, weed, and care for as needed.

Protective Herbs for the Cosmic Garden

MATERIALS:

Protective herbs of your choosing to plant near your cosmic garden

1. Plant herbs in the vicinity of the cosmic garden for protection from negative thoughts and energy, and to ward off "evil spirits." Protective herbs include betony, sage, narcissus, calendula, rue, verbena, and wormwood, *Artemisia absinthium.* These last two herbs, plus garlic and fennel, are reputed to expel negative spiritual influences.

Heaven and Earth

MATERIALS:

Supplies as needed for writing, drawing, painting, or making music—whichever form of expression you choose

1. Sit in the midst of your cosmic herb garden. Close your eyes and imagine that center as a true symbol of paradise. Now use all of your senses and imagine what an experience of paradise would be like: the sounds, sights, smells, tastes, and feelings.
2. Express your concept of paradise in words, music, or art.

Cosmic Labyrinth

MATERIALS:

> Labyrinth design
>
> Tall stake for center
>
> Plant stakes
>
> Measuring tape
>
> String
>
> Scissors
>
> Trowel
>
> Compass
>
> Herbs you choose for the theme of your labyrinth
>
> Material for surfacing the paths (grass seed, paving stones, bricks, or gravel)
>
> Journal and pencil plus art supplies, readings, and/or other materials needed for activities when you visit the labyrinth

A garden labyrinth or maze is more than a place to stroll and contemplate: the circuitous, inward path is a journey to higher levels of self-awareness and spiritual growth. Two seekers can walk the same trail while taking entirely different journeys.

1. Create a labyrinth modeled after "A Cosmic Herbal Garden" on page 121. Four paths will enter the maze and all will eventually lead to the center. Lay out the basic circle using the same approach described for "A Cosmic Herbal Garden." Paths can consist of grass, paving stones, bricks, or gravel, with beds of herbs in between the walkways. The illustration shows a basic design for a cosmic labyrinth, and you can alter this pattern or create your own.

(continued on next page)

"Cosmic Labyrinth." Enter from any of the four directions and follow
the meandering path to the center while contemplating your own spiritual journey.

2. Each time you visit your labyrinth, bring a different reading, prayer, or creative project to engage and expand your spirit. Many activities described in this book would work well, especially those in chapter 6, "Reflection and Meditation." Bring a pencil and journal to record the thoughts and revelations that come to you while navigating the labyrinth and visiting its center.

Alternative Cosmic Labyrinth for Small Yards and Rooftop Gardens

MATERIALS:

*Same as those needed for "Cosmic Labyrinth" on
page 125*

1. The labyrinth design provided consists of five concentric circles. For smaller yards in urban and suburban settings, as well as for rooftop gardens, you can remove an outer ring or two to create a more compact labyrinth.

Alternative Cosmic Labyrinth
for Apartments and Patios

MATERIALS:

Old bed sheet, blanket, or throw rug

Plastic drop cloth

Tape measure

Chalk

Paint brush

Fabric paint

Container of water

Rags for cleaning up

1. If you have an indoor setting, a patio, or other space that is too small to create a labyrinth garden, you can still enjoy the experience using a large old bed sheet, blanket or throw rug. Lay down a large plastic drop cloth, then place the sheet, blanket, or rug on top of it.
2. Use a tape measure and piece of chalk to transpose the labyrinth onto this material. Create a labyrinth with enough space that you can walk between the rows. This may entail using only three or four of the inner circles of the labyrinth design.
3. Now use a brush and fabric paint to create your labyrinth by painting the lines you have already marked with chalk.
4. Allow the labyrinth to dry while remaining on the plastic drop cloth.
5. Once the paint is dry, you can use the labyrinth as described in "Cosmic Labyrinth" on page 125.
6. When you are finished, simply roll up your labyrinth and store it until the next time you want to use it.

Cosmic Community Centerpieces

MATERIALS:

Fresh herbs and flowers of your choice from this chapter
Knife or scissors
Floral foam
Small attractive planters

ALTERNATIVE: Same as above, but use dried herbs and flowers and floral clay instead.

1 Choose some herbs and flowers and obtain them fresh from among those in the list of "Cosmic Herbs, Flowers and Fruits" in this chapter.
2. Cut the stems to length with a sharp knife or a pair of scissors.
3. Place a piece of floral foam in the bottom of several small, attractive planters. Add water to the foam to keep the herbs fresh.
4. Now push the stems of the fresh herbs into the foam to make attractive arrangements.
5. Display these arrangements on the table during the "Interfaith Manna from Heaven" potluck on page 79.

ALTERNATIVE: Create arrangements of dried flowers and substitute floral clay for the foam. Dry the herbs by hanging them upside down.

Lavender Birds of Peace

MATERIALS:

Wire clothes hanger
Fresh green stems of lavender
Thin craft wire (green)
Scissors
White glue
Empty milkweed pods

1. Lavender is a symbol of peace. Bend a wire clothes hanger into the shape of a dove.
2. Using some long, fresh green stems of lavender, fasten the ends onto the hanger with the craft wire. Use the lavender to form the shape of a bird's body, including the head, torso, and tail.
3. Glue empty milkweed pods onto the back for wings, using the delicate pointed ends as the wing tips, and position the pods so the curves swoop back like wings in flight.
4. Place or hang the bird of peace wherever you want to promote harmony.

Herbs and Flowers for

Reflection and Meditation

Agar (frankincense)
Anise
Balm
Balsam
Basil
Bergamot
Calendula
Cedar
Chamomile
Chandan (sandal-
  wood)
Cinnamon
Cypress
Dill
Frankincense
Galbanum
Hemp
Jasmine
Joe-Pye weed
Juniper

Lamb's quarters
Lavender
Marjoram
Mugwort
Myrrh
Myrtle
Onycha
Parsley
Pine
Pineapple weed
Poppy
Rose
Rue
Sage
Spikenard
Storax
Thyme
Valerian
Willow
Yarrow

6

REFLECTION AND
MEDITATION

Humankind is only grass
and its beauty like a wildflower's.
The grass withers,
the flower fades,
but the word of our God remains forever.

—Isaiah 40:6–8

I pick a sprig of parsley from the garden and enjoy its fresh, subtle taste—an essence born from the work of countless generations who have nurtured this herb, who chose to save seed from the vigorous plants and from those that possessed the most satisfying aromas and flavors. Here is not just a sprig of parsley, but a living historical record of every choice made by the herbalists who planted its antecedents, the keepers of the lineage. This simple herb has stored in its green memory the best qualities of its progenitors. Its lacy, unpretentious pale leaves express the sum of the very virtue that parsley has come to symbolize over the ages: knowledge.

Through our role in the evolution of herbs and other plants we have become cocreators of each other. Plants have, however, in their quiet way, steadfastly bent us to their wills. Each time we choose to plant the seeds from particular herbs, we act as their agents of change, creating a new generation that is stronger and more vigorous. By saving seeds and planting heirloom varieties, we perpetuate the genetic wisdom of plants.

Let the tree fall south or north—
where the tree falls,
there it lies.

—Ecclesiastes 11:3

Wandering amid the diverse array of herbs, I note how, during the night, the flower heads of many have turned to greet the morning sun. What is a plant but a fellow being whose temporal world moves at a slower pace than that of animals, we who often act in haste before fully understanding the repercussions of our actions, or even the nature of our intent?

Therein lies the wisdom of plants, which understand the virtue of simply *being,* of allowing the knowledge accrued by each generation and the vicissitudes of the environment to leave marks upon their progeny. Whether a garden herb or an ancient tree, in plants, God has given the world its true contemplatives. Their open leaves seek the light, even while roots probe the dark recesses of the soil. Plants are both yang and yin, green and complete.

HERBS OF WISDOM

What are reflection and meditation, if not pathways to truth and understanding? In Hebrew tradition, *wisdom* refers to knowledge that has grown over time, the sum of what has been learned. The flowers of herbs pollinate with others, combining their wisdom to create new expressions of qualities that have come before—unique traits of hue and scent and spice. In the true sense of the Hebrew word for *holy, kadosh,* which means "special" or "set off" from others, every new generation of herbs is holy.

Seeds of wisdom sprouted in solitude can be found in a Hindi story by the sixteenth-century writer Shaykh Manjhan, in which he tells of a king and queen who cannot bear a child. In his despair, the king goes to pray alone in a forest garden, contemplating his fate while inhaling the scents of the agar and chandan trees. In this state of meditation, the king asks for the blessing of a sage and is visited by fairies. Soon thereafter, a son, an only child, is born to the king and queen.

Through the ages, wilderness, the wild garden, has been a place to go when seeking wisdom, a vision, or spiritual guidance. When I walk through the deep woods near my Vermont home, I search for movement at the edge of my vision, an evanescent wisp of motion that is barely perceptible. It might be one of the *manôgemasak*, as the Little People are known in the homeland of the Abenaki, the Native Americans of this region, "People of the Dawn." The *manôgemasak* are always watching. If people mistreat the medicinal wild herbs—taking more than their share, wasting them, or picking the largest "Grandmother" plant—the *manôgemasak* can turn into a wasp or a black fly whose sting or bite is a reminder to always respect nature.

Why are the Little People, who are found among the traditions of indigenous peoples from around the world, often associated with herbs and flowers? And why are they always hiding just beyond the range of human vision, so much a part of our lives and yet so fleeting and elusive? In his book *al-Jami ... al-Filaha (Book of Agriculture)*, al-Ghazzi, an Islamic writer from the 1500s, observed that our spiritual selves truly are one with our environment, that within the souls of people dwell the souls of plants, animals, and minerals.

Some years ago I traveled around Scotland, sharing stories, absorbing the local lore, and carefully stowing these tales for the journey home. This is the land of the Wee Folk, the *Tuatha de Danaan*, the Celtic fairies. When humans stumble into one of their gatherings, the Wee Folk turn into herbs and flowers or butterflies so as to remain unseen. If someone "innocently" harms a butterfly's wings, or picks those flowers and hurts the Wee Folk, then bad luck will visit that person's household. Tess Darwin writes in her fascinating book *The Scots Herbal: Plant Lore of Scotland*, that foxglove takes its name from the gift of slipper-shaped flowers that the Fairy Folk wore as gloves and gave to the foxes to wear on their feet. These "folksgloves" allow foxes to hunt in wild places while making hardly a sound.

CONTEMPLATION AND MEDITATION

Myriad herbs have also traveled east to west across the sea, herbs that can enliven and enrich our lives. Herbs can aid our inner journeys as we seek to rise above the exigencies of day-to-day life. They can help us attain a state of meditation and travel beyond to a place where dreams dwell. Originally from Egypt, Asia Minor, and Greece, anise is prized for its essence of licorice. Anise seeds are burned during meditation to enhance the power of centering. When we reach a state of total relaxation, letting go of our awareness as we drift into sleep, anise helps prevent bad dreams. Cinnamon quells our anger; it calms and soothes. Valerian—relative of the biblical herb spikenard—has the power to protect us in our sleep, warding off the fears of unknown spirits in the night. A small sprig underneath the pillow will do.

We become a pure nothing
by an unknowing knowledge which is
emptiness
and solitude
and desert
and darkness
and remaining still.

—Meister Eckhart

For thousands of years, herbs have been planted in Islamic gardens, tended by people who recognize their powerful role in the realm of the spirit. Symbols that were discovered in Persia six thousand years ago, and which are similar to those in a Buddhist mandala, record an herbal vision of the cosmos sculpted in ceramic. At the center is a pool of water, a spring of life-giving force. Four beds of herb plantings radiate out from the center and reach toward the cardinal directions. There, at the center of the spiritual world, in the realm of poetry and metaphor, at the intersection of this world and paradise, these ancients sat in contemplation.

The aroma of frankincense fostered centering and meditation in these long-ago gardens. Chamomile was grown, with its hint of apples and flowers of golden hearts, bringing rest, contentment, and peace. The scent of the greenish-yellow flowers of garden rue guided the journey inward to seek self-knowledge and connect with the creative force. "Silence," Muhammad said, for "secrets are found under the white rose."

A leaf falls down from high up in the crown of an ancient willow. It spins and flutters and dances through the air as we watch it falling, falling, falling. By our feet it lands. There it will lie until the bacteria and fungi and various leaf-eating forms of life reduce it to a spindle-shaped skeleton of veins that once flowed with salicylates, the precursors to our aspirin. Willow is the wood from which magic wands are carved—it is the sacred tree of the Druids. Under its arching branches we go to sit and contemplate reflections in the water flowing past, leaning against the trunk and finding a hole where the Greeks once believed water nymphs lived. Today, willow remains a symbol of love and sorrow, reminding us of how far we have yet to travel before we will see the heart of God.

> By the rivers of Babylon
> we sat down and wept,
> when we remembered Zion.
> There on the willow trees
> we hung our harps.
>
> —Psalm 137:1–2

Christian monasticism, as a way of knowing God, began in fourth-century Egypt with Saint Anthony and other religious figures; it is an experience of God that can be attained through solitude, from prayer, and by eschewing worldly pleasures. Blessings and prayers, transformation and growth, emerge from the companion sacrifice of fasting, leading to a state of ecstasy, of transcendence. In the tradition of Jewish Kabbalah, spiritual experiences are not just centered in the realm of the spirit and intellect; they are also connected to our physical aspect, our internal realm. We dwell in our bodies. It is through the growth we seek with intention that our physical selves come to commune with the

Divine Spirit. A journey from repentance to virtue and vision awaits in the scent of the rue.

WEEDING THE BUDDHA

When I visit the herbs in our garden, I often get down on my hands and knees to gain the perspective of a small child as I examine some minute detail that has caught my eye: the curl of a leaf, the shape of a flower petal, the yellow mass of pollen on the end of a stamen where a honeybee is gathering food for the hive. Then, looking close up, I begin to notice the tiny hairs on sage leaves, the square stem of the mint, and the gently recurved leaf edges on our sweet basil, giving them the appearance of the surface of water in a glass that has been filled to a hair's breadth over the top of the rim. I reach over to the bed of thyme and nip off a few of the tiny oval leaves, hoping that a taste will yield a touch of the clarity this herb is known to impart.

Then I notice the weeds that always seem to crowd the fresh sprouts that spring from basil seed, one of the only plants I know whose seed leaves appear as perfectly formed miniatures of the leaves on the mature plant. I see the lamb's quarters has grown tall, so I reach over and yank it out, roots dangling. But this "weed" is so nutritious I could just as well be growing and eating *it*. I once prepared a plate of lamb's quarters—sautéed like spinach, along with onions and thyme. It was delicious. Which leads to the question, "What exactly is a weed?" So I ponder as I pull. Soon, one weed has led to another, and another, until the patch of basil stands clear and crisp amid the deep brown, freshly scuffed soil.

Lamb's quarters. A delicious "weed" that is a member of the spinach (goosefoot) family.

I move on to another herb bed and continue to weed. My mind wanders at first, thinking of this writing deadline I have to meet, that appointment I forgot to record in my calendar, the groceries I was asked to pick up for dinner. But then, the wheels of my mind start to slow— concerns and worries no longer catch on the threads of thought. Time passes. The call of a house wren punctures my reverie, and I realize that a span of time has passed when my mind has been still. This is what a weed is—the mantra of my garden meditation, the quiet Buddha of the herb garden. I have discovered the Zen of weeding.

On some mornings I set out with pencil and sketch pad on a journey to find some new

> *Here in this pleasant arbour by the herbs,*
> *with grape overhead,*
> *and basil in flower in the open sun,*
> *here in this quiet varied*
> *with an early summer sound of country birds,*
> *one may well muse awhile*
> *on how the soul may possess and keep*
> *her earth inheritance.*
>
> —Henry Beston, *Herbs and the Earth*

sculpture born of dew's infinitely creative hand, stringer of liquid beads that transform the familiar. Along the way, I pick and inhale the scent of some tiny yellow flowers from the heads of the aptly named pineapple weed, our local chamomile, whose dried flowers imbue a tea with a calming essence of patience and peace: the touchstones of meditation. Through the gate and down the garden path I turn toward the vigorous stalks of dill. There I drop my sit-upon and watch, cross-legged before the web of an orb-weaving spider, speckled with dew and backlit by the dazzling rays of dawn.

How can anything be more perfect? Here is such an elemental joy that I know it shares the same course as the river through which our earthly pleasures flow, emerging from experiences as seemingly divergent as the scent of warm rain, the breathtaking beauty of a ruddy sunset, or the heart-skipping pangs of love.

The light of love is appreciation; the darkness, possession. Beauty causes the heart to sing, the soul to yearn for communion with the beloved. Art is a struggle with the pulls of this duality. In this form of cocreation, we lose ourselves to the other, and the journey takes us beyond the boundaries of the self.

Inspired, I pursue this other form of meditation that is art. With pencil in hand, I softly sketch the long thick stems of dill. Emerging from a multitude of delicate strokes, the fine, ferny leaves begin to grow. There is no rush; each tiny, thread-like leaflet has to be created anew on paper. I let the dill guide me, with its power to imbue clarity of purpose. At last, my pencil swoops to trace each upward-curving stalk on which a starburst display of tiny flowers is arrayed. When I sit back, at last, and take stock of this new dill that has grown on paper, the entire head of flowers becomes the inverted frame of an umbrella, tips reaching up toward the open sky.

Before the dawn-wind rises,
before the shadows flee,
I will go to the mountain of myrrh,
to the hill of frankincense.
You are so beautiful my love,
and without a blemish.

—Song of Songs 4:6–7

Yet it is only a weak imitation of the plant I see before me. Why are we so determined to contribute our little bit of originality to the world? Perhaps it is those rare moments when we bring forth an image, a song, or a poem that is truly inspired, that contributes something new to our existence, that we sense an inkling of true creation, that we enter a true state of elation, of ecstasy. Weeding or chanting, pursuits that help us forget the "I" and the "Me," are worthwhile preludes to illustrating, carving, or molding in clay. Paradoxically, when we meld with the great Oneness, the Absolute, by transcending our own limitations, we also obtain a new level of self-awareness and new possibilities for self-realization. When we move beyond the boundaries of our self—of our bodily awareness and racing mind—there lies the world.

Weeding the Buddha—a journey of moving beyond the sensory and intellectual to become immersed in the harmonic resonance of simple being—is one of two garden paths we can take toward connecting with creation. There is the way of asceticism, but what of those days when we live so fully within our earthly beings that there seems no escape? When our intense desire to understand is manifest as an

The shell must be cracked open,
if what is inside is to come out.
If you want the kernel,
you must break the shell.
We must learn to break through things
if we are to grasp God in them.

—Meister Eckhart

insatiable sensory hunger, we can discover the heart of God in the physical world that surrounds us. This immersion often brings a desire to reflect our own vision of beauty. At those times, we can use art to reveal our experience of creation.

PERCEPTION AND PARADISE

Senses are sacred conduits for perceiving the world around us. Fragrance has been used to purify the heart of spiritual seekers in the traditional Islamic garden since medieval times. It is one pathway that can lead to an awareness of our place in creation. According to the fourteenth-century Islamic writer Abd al-Razzaq al-Qashani, these are the ways to happiness; they are our "medicine of the spirit." Calendula is a source of joy and contentment. The fragrances of marjoram, white jasmine, rose, and other herbs are equated with myriad human virtues. The olive oil that binds these scents encourages good deeds. This philosophy is grounded in the paradigm of human nature as recorded by al-Ghazzi in the book *ul-Jumi ... ul-Filuhu*, in which he says that people, as part of nature, are composed of the four elements: air, water, earth, and fire.

Herbs are an essential way for us to draw from the strength inherent in these four cornerstones of creation. Oil of lavender imparts tranquility, clear vision, and peace. Since the ancient days of Mesopotamian civilization, herbal oils have been extracted and used in massage for the same purposes that are inherent in today's practice of aromatherapy: to reduce stress, uplift the spirits, and heighten our sense of awareness.

Herbs are a little piece of heaven. When I visit my favorite shops where all things herbal are found, they are invariably designed with the same goal: to provide a world where the senses and spirit are at play. Gentle music greets my ears and delicious aromas envelop me. Soothing tabletop fountains play down into quiet pools. I look around and notice that people are quietly taking time, becoming engrossed in one fascinating find or sensory experience after another, often huddling with companions to excitedly remark on a new discovery. People who enter the shop encounter a haven of contentment, and more—delight. On one such experience I realized why this is so: herbal shops and gardens are designed to be microcosms of paradise.

> *To disfigure the rose garden,*
> *one owl alone would suffice.*
> *What fate awaits this rose garden,*
> *with all its branches decked with owls?*
>
> —Anonymous Urdu Poet, India

Herb gardens can arouse our creative spirit and incite us to pursue artistic forms of expression. To this end, herb gardens that date from the royal gardens of ancient Egypt, medieval Islamic gardens, and the cloistered gardens of Europe, to the intimate spaces nurtured by countless home herbalists of today, are all designed to block out the exigencies of our hectic and scattered lives. For 1,500 years, Islamic gardens have been built inside high walls as a shield from the dust and noise of urban streets.

Verses in the Qur'an echo memories of the *first* garden, where Adam and Eve dwelt. Paradise is found in the "Gardens of Eden underneath which

The classic rose possesses healing powers and is a symbol of love, beauty, silence, and secrets.

rivers flow" (Sura 98.8). The traditional design of Islamic gardens is that of a circle divided into quarters, with a pool of water and a pavilion in the center. The Garden of Eden itself may have inspired this design, "With the Tree of Life and the Tree of the Knowledge of Good and Evil in the middle of the garden. A river flowed from Eden to water the garden, and from there it divided to make four streams" (Genesis 2:8–10).

I saw a mighty and immeasurable
  marvelousness.
It had such a fierce shine
I could only behold it as if through a mirror.
But I knew that within it
was every manner of sweet blossoming,
every manner of good aromas and lovely scents,
it was to be enjoyed with unbounded delight.
Here were the blessed, happy ones
that moved God in their time on earth,
stirred God with sincere striving and just works.
Now in all this marvelousness,
they can enjoy the sweet ecstasy.

—Hildegard of Bingen

During the height of Victorian interest in natural history, paradise was imitated in lavish, glass-enclosed diorama gardens where stuffed wild birds perched silently on dusty branches. Often, in acknowledgment that only God can create true perfection, a stuffed snake invaded paradise and wound around the central branch in each static garden.

I have visited cloistered gardens in France and Italy, awash with varied colors from the riotous orange or purple crêpe petals of poppy to the subtle hues of lavender with its grayish-green leaves and pleasantly scented purple or pink flowers. I have walked through the wild herbs of home, brushing against the purple-spotted stems of Joe-Pye weed and stopping to pick and inhale the medicinal scent of crushed yarrow leaves; I have strolled the neat paths of countless colonial museum gardens that are lovingly restored in the yards of historic homes. Always, I want to linger and retreat from the world, then to sit quietly with an inspirational book, to say a prayer of thanks, to pull out pencil and sketch pad and grow creative roots of my own. Or, perhaps, to simply bask in a sunny nook and drift in time, absorbed in the scents and sights of that little paradise, where a gardener of herbs took more than a few moments to cultivate a bit of creation, a touch of God.

Retreat, Respite, Rose

MATERIALS:

A quiet place
Rose-scented candle, potpourri, or incense
Comfortable seat
Meditative music and player

1. Find a quiet place where you will not be disturbed.
2. Light a rose-scented candle, warm a cup of moist, rose-scented potpourri or burn some rose incense. (See the recipe for "Mesopotamian Meditation Incense" on page 151.) Rose emanates an essence that encourages silence and strengthens the will to keep important secrets.
3. Sit in a comfortable seat and softly play some meditative music. Some of my favorite CDs are: *Canticles of Ecstasy of Hildegard von Bingen*, performed by Sequentia (Deutsche Harmonia Mundi); *Chant*, by the Benedictine Monks of Santo Domingo de Silos (Angel); *Light from Assisi*, by Richard Shulman (RichHeart Music); and *A Feather on the Breath of God: Sequences and Hymns by Abbess Hildegard of Bingen* performed by Gothic Voices (Hyperion). Allow the scent of rose and the sounds of sacred music to transport you to the quiet of your own inner garden, to a visit in the heart of your private inner world.

Herbs of Meditation

MATERIALS:

Cup of chamomile tea and aniseed oil

ALTERNATIVE:

Rose oil

Leaves of mugwort

Pot of hot water

(Note: Mugwort is for inhaling and is not to be consumed.)

Meditation helps us attain higher levels of awareness and self-realization. But the ultimate experience of meditation is to transcend the self, to become one with all of creation, the Absolute. Herbs can be used to enhance a meditative experience by opening, strengthening, and vitalizing our chakras, the energy centers that run along the medial line of our bodies. Hindus and followers of other Eastern spiritual traditions recognize that our bodies have chakras, or "wheels" of light and energy. From five to twelve chakras have been described, but most traditions recognize six or seven chakras.

Meditation that engages the *Sahasrara chakra*, which is found at the top of the head, helps free the mind to connect with the essence of pure being. In some traditions, this is the *Nirvana chakra* and is symbolized by the white petals of the lotus. *Ajna*, the chakra also known as the Third Eye that resides in the center of the forehead, engages our brain, bringing us to new levels of self-awareness, self-realization, and connectedness. The chakra of the mouth, *Visshuddha*, which is found at the center of the throat, gives voice to our being and evokes wisdom of what has passed. Love, balance, wholeness, and well-being are connected to *Anahatna*, the heart chakra, which is located in the center of the chest. We can meditate on this chakra for spiritual growth and concerning forgiveness and compassion. *Manipura*, the chakra associated with the navel or solar plexus region—a focus of individual strength and intellectual

(continued on next page)

vigor—is a point of reflection for self-control over our physical wants and for maintaining a sense of humor. The lower abdomen or groin is the center of *Svadhisthana*—the chakra of emotion and passion, of sexuality and creativity—on which we can reflect to transcend sensuality and our sense of self. Finally, the elemental chakra, *Muladhara*, which is centered between the genitals and anus, ties us to Earth and focuses on our most basic needs for survival and security. Reflection on this chakra can alleviate the anxieties of daily existence and direct our energy toward attaining our full potential as physical and spiritual beings.

1. Choose the chakra you would like to focus on during your meditation.
2. Prepare some chamomile tea. By promoting peace, patience, and humility, chamomile enhances the powers of meditation.
3. Take notice of where in your body you are feeling tension. Drink the chamomile tea slowly and, with each sip, visualize the anxiety flowing from each part of your body.
4. Now take some aniseed oil and anoint the chakra that you wish to energize.
5. Sit in a relaxed position with your legs crossed, close your eyes, and try to empty your mind of thoughts, chatter, and background noise.
6. Then, begin to slowly vocalize the universal chant, *om*, drawing out each part of the voicing. In the Buddhist, Hindu, Sikh, and Jain traditions, *om* is a sacred sound that resonates with the vibration of the universe. Using deep breaths that pull air from the lower parts of your lungs, fill out each chant and evoke the sound so that is resonates from deep within your chest, reaching down to your navel. Slowly repeat this chant for about 5 minutes.
7. Meditate in the early morning, at midday, and in the evening, gradually building up from 5 to 20 minutes during each meditation.

ALTERNATIVES:

1. Substitute rose oil in place of aniseed oil during your meditations when you wish to focus on your own inner silence and on keeping close the secrets of friends and loved ones.
2. Steep some leaves of mugwort (*Artemisia vulgaris*) in a pot of hot water and inhale the steam. Essence of mugwort opens the *Ajna chakra*. **Warning: Mugwort is toxic. Do not consume in any form.**

Totality Tea

MATERIALS:

Dried leaves and flowers of bergamot (bee balm)
Pot of hot water
Tea strainer
Cup

Both our herb garden and our kitchen garden are adorned with several varieties of the hardy herb known as bergamot, or bee balm. The elegant blossoms, whose petals range from pink or red to purple and arch outward like floral fireworks, begin to open in midsummer and continue to bloom well into autumn. Watching the hummingbirds sip nectar from the long tubular petals of bergamot flowers is one of our greatest summer joys. We have some bergamot planted on each side of the pantry door, where we often stop to sniff their spicy scent.

1. Drinking bergamot tea as a prelude to meditation will help calm a restless spirit and promote serenity. Bergamot tea will foster a sense of happiness and well-being. Simply steep fresh or dried leaves and flowers in hot water for 10 minutes, then strain and serve in a cup. The edible flower also encourages the same balm-like qualities.

Art of Herbal Reflection

The list of "Herbs and Flowers for Reflection and Meditation" in this chapter is included because these herbs and flowers promote centering, peace, calm, reflection, and meditation. Here are some arts and crafts projects you can create using herbs chosen for their particular virtues.

Driftwood Herbals

MATERIALS:

Piece of driftwood that has a small hollow on top

Lump of florist's clay

Dried flowers chosen from the list of "Herbs and Flowers for Reflection and Meditation" on page 130.

ALTERNATIVE: In place of seashore driftwood use a concave stone or piece of weathered wood from a lakeshore or riverbank.

Choosing a piece of driftwood is a very personal form of creative expression. I walk along the tide line until the "spirit" of a piece beckons. I usually have to search for a long time before a piece of driftwood "speaks" to me. The crashing

"Driftwood Herbals," showing thyme along the bottom and, moving from left to right among tall plants: willow, lavender, and fir.

(continued on next page)

surf, the wind through the dune grass, and the grating of pebbles as each wave recedes back into the sea all have a soothing, hypnotic effect. As I scan the distant horizon, the ocean's primal vastness inspires a sense of awe that by comparison dwarfs my own evanescent existence.

1. Stroll along the seashore and look for a piece of driftwood in which there is a small hollow or depression.
2. Press a thick lump of florist's clay into the depression.
3. Create an arrangement composed of herbs for reflection and meditation by pushing the stems down into the clay. Be mindful to use herbs that form a pleasing combination of colors, textures, and scents.
4. Use the driftwood herbal arrangement for a centerpiece or as a specimen for the space in which you go to reflect or meditate.

ALTERNATIVE TO DRIFTWOOD HERBALS:

1. Find a concave stone or a piece of weathered wood along a riverbank or lakeshore and use that as the base for your herbal centerpiece. The shores of lakes and rivers inspire a feeling of timelessness and a sense that life is a long journey to places yet to be discovered.

Herbal Ball

MATERIALS:

Glue

Eyehook

Green Styrofoam ball about 5 inches in diameter

3 feet monofilament fishing line

Pruning clippers

Dried herbs from among the list of "Herbs and Flowers for Reflection and Meditation" on page 130

Awl, skewer, ice, or nut pick

1. Create a hanging herbal ball arrangement. Glue the threaded end of an eyehook into the Styrofoam ball.
2. Trim the stems of dried herbs to an even length of 2 or 3 inches.
3. Use an awl, skewer, or pick to poke 1-inch-deep holes into the Styrofoam that are evenly spaced about ½ inch apart over the surface of the ball.
4. Carefully insert the ends of the stems into the foam ball to form a spherical arrangement of herbs.
5. Cut several feet of monofilament fishing line and tie one end to the circle of the hook. Hang the herbal ball in your bedroom or in the space where you go to reflect or meditate. Other shapes of herbal sculptures can be made and used as centerpieces during spiritual occasions, such as Hanukkah, Christmas, Ramadan, and Kwanza.

The Art of Knowing

MATERIALS:

A favorite quiet place and a backpack or basket packed with the supplies for your chosen art project, such as drawing pen and paper, paint and brushes, clay, or a journal and pencil

1. Gather the specific materials you will need for your favorite form of artistic expression. Pack these supplies in a backpack or basket.
2. Go and sit comfortably and quietly in a spot near one of your favorite herbs.
3. Begin at the top of the herb and focus on every detail. flowers, stems, leaves and leaf hairs, colors, textures, and so on. When you feel you are beginning to truly know this plant in front of you as an individual, begin to record that knowledge in your chosen artistic form.

Seeds of Success

MATERIALS:

Seeds, dried leaves, and flowers of herbs that symbolize your chosen virtues (see "Herbs and Flowers for Reflection and Meditation" on page 130)

Construction paper

Glue

Scissors

Do you have a specific life goal that you are trying to achieve? What are you striving for in your spiritual life? Which personal qualities do you want to grow? The first step toward seeking a new way of being, or reaching a new destination, is to imagine yourself making the journey.

1. Take a long walk, go swimming, or engage in some other activity that works to open your mind's receptivity to ideas from the creative spirit. Seek a strong, beautiful image in your imagination that represents the direction you want to take in your life—your personal vision.

2. Create a collage that brings this vision to life. Gather the seeds, leaves, or dried flowers of herbs that represent the virtues you seek—the destination you desire to reach. For example, chamomile instills initiative, dill promotes clarity of purpose and fertility, rue symbolizes long life, and lavender attracts love.

3. Use construction paper, glue, and the parts of herbs you gathered as raw materials for creating your personal vision in the form of a collage. Focusing on color, texture, and shape, arrange the seeds, flower petals, and leaves to form an image of your vision. When you are satisfied with what you've created, glue the herbs in place.

4. Once the glue has dried, hang this image in your bedroom near a mirror, or in any place where you will see it often and be inspired.

Mesopotamian Meditation Incense

MATERIALS:

Coffee grinder or mortar and pestle

¼ cup loosely packed fragrant fresh or dried rose petals

1 tablespoon dry gum benzoin powder
(Gum benzoin powder is sometimes available
at craft stores or pharmacies but is easiest
to find online at www.leavesandroots.com
[look in bulk herbs under "benzoin
gum powder"].)

Rosewater

Wax paper

Cookie sheet

Matches

Incense burner

ALTERNATIVE: Use the same ingredients as above but substitute one of the following scents in place of rose petals: myrtle, frankincense, balm, hemp, pine, cedar, juniper, or cypress.

Create incense to burn during times of contemplation and meditation. Incense has been used in Syria and Palestine for more than four thousand years. "God said to Moses, 'Take sweet spices: storax, onycha, galbanum, sweet spices, and pure frankincense in equal parts, and compound an incense.... You must regard it as most holy'" (Exodus 30:34–37).

Here are some traditional aromatic herbs from ancient Mesopotamia: rose, myrtle, frankincense, balm, and hemp. Conifers were often used: pine, cedar, juniper, and cypress. The essence of frankincense promotes a meditative state. Commercial incense is available for most of these scents. Here is a recipe for making rose incense.

1. Using a coffee grinder or mortar and pestle, work ¼ cup of *fragrant*, loosely packed rose petals into a fine mash (fresh petals) or powder (dried petals).

(continued on next page)

2. Mix the mashed or powdered petals well with 1 tablespoon dried, powdered gum benzoin. Gradually add drops of rosewater and work well to create a thick paste.

3. Roll into ½-inch balls, then shape each ball into a tapered, pointed cone with a flat bottom. Set these pieces on a sheet of wax paper laid over a cookie sheet to slowly dry and cure in sunlight for one month.

4. When the incense is thoroughly dry, pick up a piece and hold it by the base of the cone. Light the pointed tip with a match, let it burn briefly, then blow it out and stand it up in an incense burner. The smoke will waft and scent the air.

ALTERNATIVE: Create incense from some of the other traditional herbs and tree scents from Mesopotamia, as listed above.

7

THE PRACTICAL REALM

There is a season for everything,
a time for every deed under heaven:
a time to be born,
a time to die,
a time to plant,
a time to harvest.

—Ecclesiastes 3:1–2

The number and variety of herbals and gardening books that have been created over time are a testament to humankind's deep, enduring relationship with plants. Placing a seed in the ground—then watering, weeding, and watching—is an elemental experience that captures the imagination in every stage of life, from the youngest child to the respected village elder.

Herbalism is an ancient pursuit. More than seven hundred years ago, a lawyer living in Bologna wrote a book called *Liber Ruralium Commodorum* or *The Book of Rural Arts*, one of the first do-it-yourself guides to country living. This treatise extolled the virtues of rural life and farming, explored the field of botany, described how to garden and care for animals, and included a section on beekeeping. About one century later, *Ménagier de Paris (The Goodman of Paris)* appeared in print. Among other topics, this detailed gardening manual described when and how to water and weed plants and even offered suggestions for pest control. Albertus Magnus's *On Vegetables and Plants*, which contained many specific practices for growing a pleasure garden replete with herbs, was first published in 1620.

PLANNING AND DESIGNING AN HERB GARDEN

Throughout time, herb gardens have appeared in many places and forms. Medieval Islamic gardens, which were grown from Spain to India, frequently sparkled with pools and fountains while plants flowed down terraces lush with green. Irrigation was commonplace in the more elaborate gardens. Gardens were planted for pleasure and for the edification of departed spirits on the grounds of mausoleums. Each day, worshipers visited raised pools in the center of mosque and *Serai* gardens—those found at inns or rest houses—to renew their faith with cleansing rituals. Indoor container gardens of potted plants were popular.

Whichever kind of design you choose, whether traditional or uniquely your own, every herb garden is a manifestation of the grower's own creative imagination and spirit. The space and resources you have to work with, however, will determine the bounds of your own expressiveness. No matter where you live—whether rural, urban, or in between—there is a form of herb gardening that will fit your situation.

Indoors

Herbs can be grown in pots, planters, and hanging baskets and placed in a sunny kitchen window or a solarium. String a trellis around a well-lit window and train climbing herbs, such as rosemary, marjoram, and borage, into a wreath of green. Choose potted herbs with desired qualities and place them in rooms where you want to encourage those specific virtues.

In our house, we place indoor herbs on a small garden cart that has several tiered shelves and can be rolled outside on mild days to let the plants gather sunshine and breathe fresh air. Here are some of the many choices for containers in which to grow herbs:

- Traditional pots
- Urns
- Hanging baskets and pots
- Half barrels
- Old washtubs and sinks
- Window boxes (indoors)

Outdoors

Instead of a traditional kitchen garden where desired herbs are grown in a plot right outside the door, plant a spirit garden in which you grow herbs for spiritual practices. Be sure to consider the particulars of each setting and how you can best use the available space to create a safe, nurturing environment for your plants.

Whether you have a large yard in the country or live in an urban environment, there are many places to grow an herb garden, including:

- Traditional garden space outdoors
- Flower bed or border
- Patio
- Rooftop
- Window box (outdoors)
- Wall (especially with tiers and ledges)
- Community garden

Most popular herbs require plenty of sunlight. Plants growing in rooftop gardens receive many hours of direct sun, but they are also exposed to desiccating winds. Extra care is required to keep rooftop plants well watered. Pots need to be heavy enough to keep the plants from blowing over, and plants must be well staked.

Design

Some of the "contemporary" practices associated with herb gardens are, in fact, drawn from old traditions. Consider the practice of using raised beds in the garden, which was touted as a new and innovative technique when it was introduced to gardeners in recent decades. Around 840 CE, however, a monk named Walahfrid Strabo, Abbot of Reichenau on Lake Constance along the border of Switzerland and Germany, wrote a book about cloister gardening called *Hortulas*, "Little Garden." Strabo's monastery grew herbs on elevated rectangular beds that were framed with wooden planks.

The first monastic community, which was started by Saint Anthony in the fourth century, had its own garden, as did a Benedictine monastery that formed two hundred years later. One large medieval monastic garden from the Benedictine Abbey of Saint Gall in Switzerland consisted of eighteen rectangles, each of which measured five feet wide and twenty-five feet long. The original recorded design for this ninth-century garden still exists and is considered the oldest surviving garden plan. A Celtic monk named Saint Fiacre, who tilled the soil in the village of Meaux in northern France, so personified this greening of monastic life that he became the patron saint of the garden.

Four walls surrounded the garden of Saint Gall. Cloister gardens were enclosed in order to create spaces for quiet contemplation. Many different borders can be used to create a space for your herb garden that sets it apart from its environs, such as an arbor, a fence, a hedge, a wall, or a trellis.

The use of space is critical when planning your herb garden. Go outside and measure the perimeter of the area you plan to use. Draw this boundary on paper and create an initial sketch of the garden design that you have in mind. This is the time to let your creativity run free, to consider such plant qualities as color, texture, scent, and height. Think of

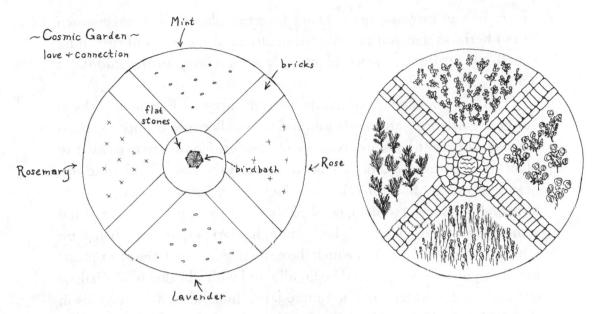

Planning "A Cosmic Herbal Garden" on the theme of love and connection. Complementary pairs of herbs include mint (passion) and lavender (peace); rose (love) and rosemary (fidelity).

this initial sketch as a form of artwork —a combination of painting and sculpting with plants while also considering their olfactory delights. If you are planting a patio or rooftop garden, or simply potting herbs indoors, create a plan for how you want to arrange herbs in different pots as well as within larger containers such as urns and barrels.

Once you have set a clear design down on paper, it is time to plan how you will transform that design into a pleasing herb garden. On a clean sheet of paper, create an appropriate scale and use a ruler to carefully plot a detailed picture of how you want the garden to be laid out on the ground. Include specific measurements for the sizes of each plant bed, for the distances between beds, and for other considerations, such as how the beds will align with the four directions or how plants can be arranged to form a mandala design (see "A Cosmic Herbal Garden" in chapter 5). Within each bed that you have delineated on paper, record the recommended distances between seedlings and seeds so that plants will have ample room to grow. As a rule, allot each perennial plant about one square foot of growing space. Don't forget to plan paths to access each bed of herbs so that you are not continually bending over and stretching your back in order to reach plants that are growing in the middle of a bed.

Paths can be made from many different surfaces. The main paths in our herb garden are carpets of grass and the smaller, interconnecting trails between different beds are made of old bricks. I have often wanted to plant some paths as chamomile lawn, to smell the sweet, apple-like fragrance of this gentle herb, *Chamaemelum nobile*. Paths can also be made of gravel, sand, colored sand, crushed shells, or by laying a surface of flat stones. If your garden space is large enough, mark a space for a bench on which to rest—a place from which the garden would look the most pleasing. The garden's center could be highlighted with a birdbath, sundial, or statue. Large gardens could accommodate a four-sided, arched trellis in the center on which climbing herbs and flowers are trained.

When you are ready to mark the garden outdoors, bring your detailed garden plan and a pencil, roll of heavy string, package of small bamboo stakes, small bag of lime, small plastic container, scissors, tape measure, and, if desired, a compass. Carefully measure and outline the garden by scooping some lime into the container and sprinkling it atop the soil. Then use the stakes to mark the boundaries of paths in order to avoid stepping on, and compacting, the soil where plants will grow. Cut pieces of string to mark the margins of planting beds. Once you have mapped out the entire garden on the ground, you may need to make minor design adjustments so everything fits harmoniously. Be sure to record these changes on the master garden plan.

Choosing and Obtaining Herbs for Your Garden

The satisfaction you derive from an herb garden will be enhanced by choosing the kinds of herbs you enjoy and the particular varieties that will thrive in your local climate and growing conditions. Fortunately, there are many excellent sources of herbs, and growers who are both passionate and knowledgeable about how and where to best grow them.

Choosing Herbs

Before you begin choosing herbs for your garden, find out which plant hardiness zone you live in. These standardized zones mark the regions in which growing seasons are of a particular duration. Whether you are planting seeds, seedlings, or larger plants, check the "days to maturity" and choose herb varieties that will mature within the length of your growing season. Most seed catalogs contain a map of plant hardiness zones.

If you want to grow varieties of herbs that require a milder climate and longer growing season than you experience locally, try planting in pots. Simply keep the potted plants inside during the cool time of year and move them outside for the warm season. When springtime arrives, acclimate these plants to the outdoors by increments, exposing them to gradually longer periods outside each day. Hibiscus responds very well to this practice, and you could even grow a young bay laurel tree. This is an excellent method for managing the ubiquitous mint. Take pots of mint outdoors and bury them in the garden during the summer, then dig them up and bring them inside when cold weather returns. This will also prevent mint from spreading throughout the garden.

Although it is possible to control the amount of water your herbs receive, it is not feasible to alter the growing conditions themselves without investing a lot of time, effort, and resources. Look at the basics that you have to work with: sunlight, soil, and space. It will be easier, in the long run, to choose herbs that grow well in the natural conditions at hand, rather than struggling to get plants to thrive in an environment they're not suited for. This maxim also holds true for the placement of the particular herbs you choose to grow. In order to assure that plants obtain enough sunlight, place taller herbs in the center of the plant beds and shorter varieties in front. Otherwise, you will be constantly pruning away healthy foliage to create light and space for herbs that are getting crowded out.

When choosing herbs to buy, look the plants over carefully. Appearance is an indicator of health and vigor. Pick plants that look hardy, have good color, and are free of diseases and insect pests. Organically grown herbs offer the healthful benefit of being grown without harmful chemicals, which can leave residues on food and damage the environment.

Most herbs will grow well together, but certain varieties are not compatible and need to be separated. When fennel and dill are grown in close proximity, they tend to cross-pollinate, diluting their distinct flavors and aromas. Wormwood inhibits the growth of some herbs, including sage, anise, fennel, and caraway, and so needs to be planted away from those varieties. Competitive plants like bee balm need to be planted in their own space to prevent them from overtaking others.

As you consider which plants you want to include in your herb garden, always think of how you would like them to be arranged. A well-designed garden is a place where the qualities of leaf, stem, and flower are complementary. You can also focus on herbs whose flowers and foliage emanate your favorite aromas.

Here are some physical factors to keep in mind when planning your herb garden:

- Color
- Texture
- Height and spread at maturtiy
- Scent
- Timing of blooms

If you have chosen a particular purpose or theme for your herb garden, now is the time to select herbs that will fulfill that vision. You may want to include herbs that focus on particular virtues, healing qualities, or spiritual traditions, such as Native American faiths, Judaism, Christianity, Islam, Hinduism, or Buddhism.

The aforementioned cloister garden of Saint Gall contained several fountains, fruit and nut trees, and specialized plots for culinary and healing herbs. Medicinal herbs included basil, sage, rue, mint, rose, lily, fennel, boneset, soapwort, and selfheal. The kitchen garden grew onion, dill, coriander, leek, and garlic. And, some 1,200 years ago, the meticulous gardeners of Saint Gall maintained a practice that is still highly recommended: they drew a detailed plan of the garden grounds on which all of the plant names were labeled.

Herbs associated with other spiritual traditions can be found throughout this book. For example, here is just a sampling of herbs that were grown in historic Islamic gardens: basil, calendula, caraway, chamomile, chrysanthemum, citrus, cumin (white and black), dill, fennel, ginger, henna, hibiscus, jasmine, mallow, marigold, mint, narcissus, oleander, oregano, plumeria, rose, thyme, violet, and wormwood (Artemesia).

Some powerful healing herbs: fennel (tall and center) and (bottom left to right) basil, summer savory, and ginger root.

Obtaining Herbs

The easiest way to acquire herbs is to purchase seeds and seedlings from a local farmer's market, garden store, or plant nursery. These herb sources tend to carry specific varieties that will grow well in your local climate. Fortunately, plant nurseries are one of the few remnants of historic agricultural economies in many regions, even in places where the land is now mostly devoted to urban and suburban uses. The survival of these businesses is a clear sign of how important gardening is to residents in every kind of community. Purchasing seeds and plants from local growers and nurseries supports the local economy and enhances a sense of community.

In time, you will discover that many people who live nearby cultivate a great variety of herbs. Early spring is a good time of year to attend local "plant swaps," during which growers bring pots of herbs to trade for other varieties. If you don't currently have a plant swap in your area, you could start one. Many of the plants exchanged at plant swaps are divided from long established beds of herbs.

Still, you may not be able to obtain all of the herbs you want or need locally. A plethora of mail-order catalogs exists from which you can order herb seeds and seedlings. There are also many sites on the Internet; simply conduct a web search using the key words "herb supply." See the appendix for a list of helpful resources.

PREPARING THE SOIL

Soil is the medium from which all herbs spring. Healthy soil grows vigorous plants that have strong resistance to insect pests and diseases. A good herbal potting-soil mix consists of three parts garden soil; one part peat, compost, or aged manure; and one part sand. This will provide healthy soil structure, good nutrition, and adequate drainage.

The earth is at the same time mother—
she is mother of all that is natural,
mother of all that is human.
She is the mother of all,
for contained in her are the seeds of all.
The earth of humankind contains all moistness,
all verdancy, all germinating power.
It is in so many ways fruitful.

—Hildegard of Bingen

Many popular herbs require well-drained soil, whether they are growing in a garden or in containers. Put some soil in a pot that has drainage holes in the bottom, and, if indoors, place in a waterproof tray. If a pot has an enclosed bottom, be sure to include 2 or 3 inches of gravel under the soil to create a space into which water can drain. Always be careful not to water too heavily, and never put an enclosed pot outdoors where it can fill with rainwater and drown the roots.

Consult your local plant nursery about the specific kind of soil needed for each of the herbs you obtain, as well as for other herbs you plan to grow. Many local nursery growers possess a great deal of knowledge about the culture and growing needs of the plants they sell and are usually enthusiastic about sharing their expertise with customers.

Whenever planting or transplanting herb seedlings outdoors, I dig the hole and add a dash of compost and bone meal for tilth, drainage, and nutrients. Many popular herbs prefer a soil that is somewhat alkaline, so adding a tablespoon or two of agricultural lime helps the roots to better absorb nutrients. I mix all of this thoroughly into the soil at the bottom of the hole.

Caring for Plants

Certain herbs do well when started indoors, including basil, borage, marjoram, oregano, chamomile (German), catnip, sorrel, and thyme. Plant the seeds in flats containing well-drained, airy soil with lots of organic matter. Borage and sorrel, however, prefer soil that is moist and rich.

Some Native American cultures, such as the Tewas of the Rio Grande, plant seeds

For see, winter is past,
the rains are over and gone.
The flowers appear on the earth.
The season of glad songs has come.

—Song of Songs 2:11–12

when the moon is waxing—in the part of its cycle when it becomes larger each night. This way, the seeds and seedlings can draw on the strength of the growing moon. Many other cultures also plant most herbs with the growing moon, but they plant root-yielding herbs, such as ginger and comfrey, during the new moon.

When seedlings are about 4 inches tall and the weather is warm enough to transplant, introduce them gradually to the outdoors so they can adjust. This is called *hardening off.* Start by putting the flats outside in a partly shady place for a few hours on the first day, a half-hour longer on the second day, and so on. Gradually expose the plants to longer periods of direct sunshine each day. Once the plants have become acclimated and the danger of frost is past, store the flats on a porch, in a garage, or in some other sheltered place at night.

As the garden soil warms and becomes dry enough to plant, gently remove each seedling from its flat while keeping the clump of soil that is attached to the roots intact. Always keep the roots damp. If the roots are bound into a tangle, carefully tease loose the ones on the bottom of the soil mass. In order to subject the seedlings to as little stress as possible, transplant in the cool of the morning, on a cloudy day, or in early evening after the heat of the sun has passed. Water transplants daily for about two weeks, then as needed.

Keep seedlings weeded and well fed, but don't overfertilize. A monthly side dressing of compost mixed with well-aged manure will grow vigorous herbs that produce a strong essence. Manure from cattle, sheep, or horses will do. A diet that is too rich results in tall, leggy plants and reduces the potency of essential oils.

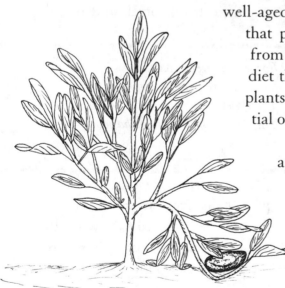

Once the seedlings grow to around 6 inches tall, some growers like to spread a light mulch around the base of the plants. Mulch feeds the soil, helps retain moisture, and cuts down on weeds. I use field hay in our vegetable garden, but well-shredded leaves or grass clippings or cocoa hulls will do. If you live

Healing in or *layering* for plant propagation. After a few months, sufficient roots will form on the buried portion of stem (right) to trim off the new growth and transplant.

in a region that receives frequent rainfall, however, mulch can harbor mold and mildew spores that can afflict some herbs, such as basil. For this reason, here in the moist summer climate of the Northeast, I prefer to maintain bare soil under our herbs so that the surface of the soil remains dry and well aerated. In the arid Southwest, however, where molding is not a critical concern and water is in short supply, mulching is a good management practice. When the growing season ends, I cover sensitive perennial herbs with a thick layer of mulch to shelter their roots from extreme cold.

After your perennial herbs have become established, you can propagate new plants by *root division*, by *cuttings*, and through a process called *healing in* or *layering*. Division entails taking a spade or shovel and working the roots free from a clump of densely growing herbs for planting elsewhere. Cuttings are more involved. In spring or autumn, take a long woody shoot from the plant by cutting at an angle close to the ground. Remove leaves from the base of this shoot, coat it with rooting powder, then pot it in a light soil mix and keep well watered. For layering, simply bend a long woody shoot and bury the middle of that stem under a few inches of soil and hold it down with a small rock. Within a month or two the cutting or healed-in stem will have developed its own root system and be ready to transplant.

HARVESTING AND PRESERVING HERBS

What can you do once your labor of love has produced a healthy, plentiful crop? The timing of the harvest, as well as proper techniques for curing and preserving, are the keys to a satisfying store of potent, aromatic herbs.

Harvesting

There are many beliefs about how best to harvest herbs. Hildegard of Bingen asserted that medicinal plants held their greatest potency if picked when the moon was waxing. She also wrote that herbs that will be preserved for a long time should be harvested during the waning moon. In many parts of the world, however, herbs are gathered in the full moon when the sap, and the strength of the oils, are on the rise. In fact, seasons *do* determine the optimal time for "bringing in." Roots and rhizomes—such as ginger, ginseng, and mandrake—are best when harvested in early spring or late autumn, when the plants have reserved much of their energy and essence below ground. Dig widely around the plant to avoid cutting the roots. Wash roots with cold water and dry thoroughly.

> *See'st then not that*
> *God sends down rain from the sky?*
> *With it we then bring out produce*
> *of various colors.*
>
> —Sura 35:27

The essence of a plant becomes concentrated each night, so herbs are most potent when picked in early morning before the sun's heat and light dissipate the essential oils. Harvesting is best when done on a clear, dry morning just after the dew has left the leaves, but not after heavy rains or watering. Substances in the leaves and stems also lose their strength after blooming, when plants focus their energy on flowers and seeds. Most herbs should be harvested just before flowering. Use sharp pruning clippers so as not to tear the stems. If you don't cut too low on the stem, many herbs, such as basil, will produce additional growth for harvest.

You may want to choose several individual plants and allow their flowers to produce seeds for next year's crop. Just before the seeds have matured, invert a paper bag over each flower and tie the mouth of the bag with string. Once the seeds have matured, cut off each seed head with the bag attached. Turn the bag right side up, tap the seeds into the bag, and then remove the string and plant.

Preserving

Herbs need to be stored properly to keep them safe and dry; to preserve the potency of the essential oils in their leaves, stems, and roots; and to allow the seeds to germinate during the next growing season. *Be sure to clearly label every jar, bag, or other container, including the name of the contents and the date of harvest.*

The leaves and flowers of herbs should be preserved fresh, immediately after harvesting. It is best to use a clean cloth and carefully dust off the leaves, without getting them wet. If you must wash them, spin the water out of them in a lettuce spinner, and then hang them to dry immediately. If you plan to use the herbs fresh, and within the next few weeks, place them in plastic bags and refrigerate. Otherwise, fresh herbs can be frozen for long-term storage in plastic freezer bags. Herbs that freeze especially well include parsley, dill, chives, mint, oregano, marjoram, tarragon, lovage, and sorrel.

If you plan to dry the herbs for long-term storage, clean them and tie the ends of the stems into bundles of five to ten. I find it is easier to use light rubber bands to hold the bundles together, which also keeps them from loosening up as the drying stems shrink. Hang the bundles in a warm, dry space that is clean and well ventilated. You can suspend them directly from beams or attach them to heavy string that runs across the ceiling. To maintain the distinct aromas and flavors of each type of herb, string only one kind in each bundle and keep them from coming into contact with other varieties. Catch any falling seeds by placing a piece of muslin below. *Always keep drying herbs out of the sunlight and away from high heat because these will drive off the volatile essential oils.*

If you don't have a good, out-of-the-way space for hanging small bundles of herbs to dry, simply lay the stalks from each type of herb on a piece of cheesecloth or muslin. Once the herbs have begun to lose their moisture and are beyond the danger of mildewing, gather up each piece of muslin by the corners and tie the corners together to form a sling. Hanging these larger bundles will take up less space and be less messy.

Leaves will have become dry enough if they crackle and crush when squeezed. Be careful not to overdry herbs or the leaves will become powdery and lose their potency. Store herbs in a cupboard in airtight jars. If you want to experience the full essence of your herbs, store the leaves whole and crush only the amount you need each time you use them.

I like to use a small coffee grinder, but a mortar and pestle will do. For each kind of herb, it is always good to keep some whole leaves on hand for use in making teas, infusions, holiday decorations, sachets, potpourris, and other herbal creations.

Preserve seeds by spreading them one layer thick on pans or dishes, then covering with a clean cloth. Place the seeds in a warm, dry place for two to four weeks. Large, fleshy seeds, such as rose hips, should be turned once each day. After the seeds have become dry and hard to the touch, put them in clean, clear glass jars away from sunlight. Seal the jars, but not airtight, and store these in a cool, dry place that is well ventilated.

Roots that have been harvested and cleaned need to be heated to drive off the moisture deep inside. Place the roots on flat pans and dry them in an oven set at 120°F until they become brittle. Turn the roots at intervals while they are drying. After the dried roots have cooled, place them in glass jars that are opaque and airtight. Store in a cool place and out of the sunlight. Some roots, like those of ginger, can also be frozen.

By planning and designing your own herb garden and growing interesting varieties, you will develop a deep sense of appreciation for the intriguing bouquet of herbs that come from around the world. As herbs grow, their array of sensory delights reflects the rich cultures and spiritual traditions as well as the diverse environments in which the history of each plant is rooted.

The mandrakes yield their fragrance, the rarest fruits are at our doors.

—Song of Songs 7:14

The daily care that you provide—the watering, weeding, and feeding of tender shoots—will cultivate a close bond between you and your plants. In time, your perceptions will evolve, heightening your awareness of the plants' remarkable scents, colors, textures, and blossoms. Careful picking and processing are the final steps toward fully appreciating the fruits of your labor: a harvest of fine herbs that holds endless promise for enriching your spiritual practices.

APPENDIX:
SOURCES FOR HERBS,
SEEDS, AND HERBAL SUPPLIES

Sources for herbs can be found among members of the following organizations:

American Herb Association
P.O. Box 1673
Nevada City, CA 95959
Phone: (530) 265-9552
www.ahaherb.com

Herb Research Foundation
4140 15th Street
Boulder, CO 80304
Phone: (303) 449-2265
www.herbs.org

Herb Society of America
9019 Kirtland Chardon Road
Kirtland, OH 44094
Phone: (440) 256-0514
www.herbsociety.org

A wealth of sources for herbs, essential oils, herbal craft supplies, and related materials can be found at this web-link hub: www.google.com/Top/Shopping/Health/Alternative/Herbs.

Sources for Native Heirloom Seeds

Seeds may be purchased through heirloom seed catalogs, from a seed saver's exchange, or from a source of traditional Native American crops. Here are some recommended Native seed sources that stock a variety of herbs:

Seeds of Change
P.O. Box 15700
Santa Fe, NM 87592
Phone: (505) 438-8080
www.seedsofchange.com

Seeds of Change has educational resources available as well as films and information about upcoming conferences. There is also a Seeds of Change garden website with lots of information about the history of herbs and spices: www.mnh.si.edu/archives/garden/history/herbs.html.

Native Seeds/SEARCH
526 N. Fourth Avenue
Tucson, AZ 85705
Phone: (866) 622-5561
www.nativeseeds.org

Native Seeds/SEARCH also has available video recordings, slides, and curriculum materials that teach about the work of finding and preserving native seeds in the Southwest, as well as their work using native crops of the Southwest to control diabetes.

Eastern Native Seed Conservancy
P.O. Box 451
Great Barrington, MA 01230
Phone: (413) 229-8316
www.enscseeds.org

The Eastern Native Seed Conservancy is working to preserve, propagate, and distribute both native and nonnative heirloom varieties, with an emphasis on the seeds of eastern and northern plants. In addition to distributing seeds to eastern Native peoples, the Eastern Native Seed Conservancy has established a general seed-saver's network called the Conservation and Regional Exchange by Seed Savers (CRESS).

General Sources for Herbs and Heirloom Seeds

Abundant Life Seeds
P.O. Box 157
Saginaw, OR 97472-0157
Phone: (541) 767-9606
www.abundantlifeseeds.com

Bountiful Gardens
18001 Shafer Ranch Road
Willits, CA 95490
Phone: (707) 459-6410
www.bountifulgardens.org

Companion Plants
7247 North Coolville Ridge Road
Athens, OH 45701
Phone: (740) 592-4643
www.companionplants.com

Companion Plants stocks some six hundred varieties of seeds and plants for medicinal, culinary, and aromatic herbs, including many traditional Native American varieties.

Garden City Seeds
P.O. Box 307
Thorp, WA 98946
Phone: (509) 964-7000
www.gardencityseeds.net

Seed Savers Exchange
3094 N. Winn Road
Decorah, IA 52101
Phone: (563) 382-5990
www.seedsavers.org

The members of Seed Savers Exchange plant and preserve more than five thousand varieties of heirloom seed stocks.

Southern Exposure Seed Exchange
P.O. Box 460
Mineral, VA 23117
Phone: (540) 894-9480
www.southernexposure.com

GLOSSARY AND INDEX
OF HERBS AND FLOWERS

Herbs can be challenging to identify by common names even when those names are the ones we use today. This book includes the names of herbs that go back for several thousand years. Wherever the identity of a particular plant is certain, this glossary simply provides the common and Latin name. In cases where the common name of a plant has several connotations, or where the name has had different meanings through time, the possibilities are discussed.

Page numbers in bold refer to illustrations.

173

Celandine: *Chelidonium majus*. See pages 86, **93.**

Celery, sweet: *Apium dulce*. See pages 8, 11.

Celery, wild: *Apium graveolens*. See pages 8, 11.

Chamomile: *Chamaemelum nobile* (*Anthemis nobilis*) is a short perennial that is also known as Roman chamomile. German chamomile, *Matricaria recutita*, is an annual that grows up to three feet tall. See pages 8, 10, 20, 32, 34, 47, 86, 90, 93, 104, 107, 110, 114, 118, 130, 135, 137, 143, 144, 150, 158, 161, 163.

Chandan: *See* sandalwood.

Chervil: *Anthriscus cerefolium*. See page 8.

Chicory: *Cichorium intybus*. See pages 8, 34, 86, 90.

Chili: *Capsicum annuum*. See page 58.

Chives: *Allium schoenoprasum*. See pages 8, **36,** 54, 60, 167.

Chrysanthemum: *Chrysanthemum species*. See page 161.

Cinnamon: *Cinnamomum zeylanicum*. See pages 3, 7, 8, 11, 27, 29, 34, 39, 42, 43, 54, 58, 60, **61,** 71, 79, 80, 83, 85, 86, 89, 100, 104, 105, 130, 134.

Citron: *Citrus medica*. See pages 8, 34, 54, 63, 85.

Citrus: In the text, citrus is mentioned as part of a historic Islamic garden. The varieties of citrus that would have been grown include the Seville or sour orange, *Citrus aurantium*; grapefruit, *Citrus maxima*; Chinese lemon, *Citrus limonia mayeri*; citron lemon, *Citrus medica*; and *Citrus bigarradia*, which has large aromatic white flowers that are preferred for making perfume. See page 161.

Clematis: *Clematis species*. See pages 86, 96.

Clove: *Syzygium aromaticum* (*Eugenia aromatica*). See pages 8, 11, 12, 20, 25, 26, 30, 32, 34, 45, 54, **61,** 71, 74, 83, 85, 86, 104, 105.

Clover, red: *Trifolium pratense*. See pages 86, **93,** 107, 110, 118.

Clover, white: *Trifolium repens*. See pages 86, 93, 107, 110, 118.

Coriander: *Coriandrum sativum*. See pages 8, 12, 34, 37, 54, 59, 80, 161.

Corn: *Zea mays*. See pages 2, 14, 88, 110.

Cornflower: *Centaurea cyanus*. Varieties of this popular garden flower produce blossoms of blue, white, pink, or purple. See pages 54, 85, 86, 96.

Cornflower, blue: *See* Cornflower.

Cumin: *Cuminum cyminum*. Also known as white cumin. See pages 8, 10, 12, 54, 58, 86, 92, 108, 161.

Cypress: *Cupressus species*. See pages 130, 151.

Daisy, oxeye: *Chrysanthemum leucanthemum*. See pages 86, **93.**

Dandelion, common: *Taraxacum officinale*. See pages 86, **102,** 110, 118.

Dates, Date palm: *Phoenix dactylifera*. See pages 4, 58, 77.

Delphinium: *Delphinium species*. See pages 54, 84.

Juniper: *Retama raetam*. This is most likely the biblical "juniper" or *rethem*. It is really a kind of broom—white broom. See pages 130, 151.

Juniper, common: *Juniperus communis*. This is the low-growing juniper of temperate regions. See pages 130, 151.

Lamb's quarters: *Chenopodium album*. See pages 86, 93, 130, **136.**

Larkspur: *Delphinium species*. See pages 54, 84.

Lavender: *Lavandula angustifolia*. See pages 8, 20, 21, 22, 23, 28, 33, 34, **36,** 39, 42, 70, 85, 96, 107, 110, 114, 117, 122, 129, 130, 139, 141, **147,** 150, **157.**

Leek: *Allium porrum*. See pages 54, 59, 161.

Licorice: *Glycyrrhiza glabra*. See pages 8, 134.

Lily, Madonna: *Lilium candidum*. See pages 8, 20, 86, 96, 110, 118, 161.

Lily, white: *Lilium species*. See pages 8, 20, 86, 96, 110, 114, 161.

Lotus: *Nelumbo nucifera*. The Indian lotus or sacred lotus, and other species. See pages 54, 84, 86, 90, 96, 110, 114, 115, 143.

Lotus, night-opening or Egyptian lotus: *Nymphaea lotus*. See page 114.

Lovage: *Levisticum officinale*. See pages 8, 11, 167.

Lupine: *Lupinus polyphyllus*. See pages 86, 96.

Mallow: *Malva species*. See page 161.

Mandrake: *Mandragora officinarum*. See pages 7, 86, 106, 107, 166, 168.

Maple, striped: *Acer pensylvanicum*. See pages 8, 18.

Marigold: *Calendula officinalis*. (*See also* Calendula.) See pages 8, 28, 49, 86, 102, 110, 118, 123, 130, 139, 161.

Marjoram, sweet: *Origanum majorana*, L. or *Majorana hortensis*. Marjoram is also believed to be the plant referred to as hyssop in the Bible. See pages 8, 20, 22, 33, 34, **36,** 37, 47, 86, 91, 101, 107, 110, 114, 117, 130, 139, 154, 163, 167.

Milkweed: *Asclepias species*. See pages 8, 18, 129.

Milkwort, common: *Polygala vulgaris*. This widespread European herb was reputed to stimulate breast milk. *Milkwort* means, "milk plant". See pages 110, 118.

Mint: *Mentha species*. See pages 8, 11, 12, 20, 25, 33, **36,** 34, 37, 49, 54, 81, 86, 104, 107, 110, 114, 122, 136, **157,** 159, 161, 167.

Miswak: *Salvadora persica*. See pages 4, 54, 58.

Mugwort: *Artemisia vulgaris*. See pages 143, 145.

Musk. Not an herb at all, traditional Islamic musk was taken from the scent glands of the Siberian musk deer (*Moschus moschiferus*), which is now a vulnerable species. Most musk is produced synthetically today. See pages 20, 34, 40, 86, 91.

Mustard (Mustard tree): There is much conjecture as to which plant Christ refers to in his parable of the mustard seed (Matthew 13:31–32; Mark 4:31–32; Luke 13:19 and

Plumeria, Indian jasmine or Frangipani: *Plumeria alba.* See page 161.

Polypody, fern: *Polypodium vulgare.* See page 8.

Pomegranate: *Punica granatum.* See pages 3, 110, 114.

Poppy: *Papaver species.* Any of the poppies found in Egypt, Europe, and the Middle East. There are about one hundred species in all. See page 54, 84, 86, 96, 130, 141.

Poppy, red: Red-flowered poppy, field poppy, or corn poppy, *Papaver rhoeas. See* Poppy.

Queen Anne's lace: *Daucus carota.* See page **93.**

Romaine lettuce: *Lactuca sativa longifolia.* See pages 54, 60, 79.

Rose: *Rosa species.* See page 8, 11, 20, 25, 28, 34, 38, 39, 40, 42, 43, 54, 70, 75, 76, 85, 86, 98, 104, 106, 107, 110, 114, 118, 122, 130, 135, 139, **140,** 142, 143, 145, 151, **157,** 161, 168.

Rosemary: *Rosmarinus officinalis.* See pages 8, 21, **22,** 25, 28, **36,** 54, **56,** 64, 70, 85, 86, 89, 98, 107, 110, 122, 154, **157.**

Rosewater: Fragrant essence of rose captured by infusing petals in water or by distillation. See page 4, 40, 54, 58, 85, 91, 151, 152.

Rowan or rowen tree: *Sorbus aucuparia.* See pages 110, 119.

Rue. *See* Garden rue.

Saffron: The dried stigmas (upper female flower parts) of *Crocus sativus.* See pages 3, 7, 8, 20, 34, 39, 54, 58, 114.

Saffron crocus: *Crocus sativus.* See pages 7, 86, 91, 110.

Sage (North America): There are several of species native to the West and Southwest, including white sage, *Salvia apiana*; purple sage, *S. dorii*; and black sage, *S. mellifera.* See pages 2, 8, 14, 15, 16, 23, 24.

Sage (southern Europe): *Salvia officinalis.* See pages 2, 8, 14, **15,** 16, 23, 24, **36,** 37, 54, 81, 86, 90, 107, 110, 122, 123, 130, 133, 136, 160, 161, **164.**

Sandalwood: *Santalum album.* See pages 8, 30, 33, 34, 39, 47, 51, 52, 110, 114, 130.

Savory: *See* Savory, summer.

Savory, summer: *Satureja hortensis.* See pages 8, 54, 110, 119, **161.**

Selfheal: *Prunella vulgaris.* See page 161.

Snapdragon: *Antirrhinum majus.* See pages 86, 96.

Soapwort: *Saponaria officinalis.* See page 161.

Sorrel, garden or common: *Rumex acetosa.* See pages 8, 107, 163, 167.

Spearmint: *Mentha spicata.* See pages 49, 86, 104, 107.

Spikenard: *Nardostachys jatamansi.* This aromatic biblical herb is a member of the valerian family. It is to be distinguished from the North American spikenard, *Aralia racemosa.* See pages 3, 130, 134.

Star anise: *Illicium verum.* The star anise tree of eastern Asia bears anise-scented, star-shaped fruit. See pages 54, 85.

Sumac: *Rhus species*. In northeastern North America, sumac fruit is used for making tea from among the species that produce *red* berries. ***Caution:* Never touch or ingest the poisonous *white* berries of poison sumac, *Rhus vernix.*** See pages 8, 18.

Sunflower: *Helianthus annuus*. See pages 14, 54, 62.

Sweetfern: *Comptonia peregrina*. See pages 8, 18, 54.

Sweetgrass: *Hierochloe odorata*. See pages 54, 70.

Tamarind: *Tamarindus indica*. See page 34.

Tansy: *Tanacetum vulgare*. See pages 8, 35, **36,** 39, 54.

Tarragon: *Artemesia dracunculus*. See page 167.

Thyme: *Thymus species*, particularly common or garden thyme, *Thymus vulgaris*. See pages 8, 20, 27, 34, 35, **36,** 37, 45, 54, 74, 81, 86, 100, 110, 114, 130, 136, 147, 161, 163.

Tobacco: *Nicotiana species*, especially *Nicotiana tabacum*. This is the ceremonial plant used widely by Native Americans. The Abenaki peoples discussed in this book have used this plant historically, but it is uncertain how far back in time the use of tobacco originated in the Northeast. Tobacco is to be distinguished from Indian tobacco, *Lobelia inflata,* which some believe tastes like regular tobacco, but does not contain nicotine. Indian tobacco is a powerful healing herb that must be used with the care and advice of an expert. See pages 2, 8, 14, 54, 62.

Turmeric: *Curcuma longa*. See pages 54, 58, 110, 115.

Valerian: *Valeriana officinalis*. See pages 130, 134.

Verbena: *Verbena species*. A number of plants in this widespread genus with brightly colored flowers are from the Americas and are called "verbena." Verbena is also used to describe the aromatic lemon verbena, *Aloysia triphylla (Lippia citriodora)*, which is indigenous to South and Central America. The verbena that is referred to in this book is the European verbena, or vervain (*V. officinalis*). See pages 8, 54, 110, 123.

Vervain: *Verbena officinalis*. This European plant is sometimes called verbena. See pages 107, 110, 119.

Violet: *Viola species*. See pages 8, 11, 25, 34, 42, 43, 54, 71, 85, 86, 103, 106, 107, 110, 114, 161.

White cumin: *See* cumin.

Wild marjoram: *Origanum vulgare*. Oregano. See pages 8, 54.

Wild thyme: *Thymus serpyllum*. See pages 8, 11, 54.

Willow: *Salix species*. Willows are found worldwide. The only specific willow referred to in this book is the willow of Babylon or weeping willow, *Salix babylonica* (Psalm 137:1–2). See pages 7, 8, 14, 18, 30, 31, 54, 63, 110, 119, 130, 135, **147.**

Wormwood: *Artemisia absinthium*. See pages 8, 10, 54, 86, 90, 110, 123, 160, 161.

Yarrow: *Achillea millefolium*. This powerful healing herb is a native to Europe and western Asia. It is an important plant used by indigenous healers in North America, many of whom consider it a native species. See pages 8, 9, 10, 54, 110, 118, 130, 141.

INDEX OF ACTIVITIES

CREDITS

We are grateful for permission to include the following: The quotes from Hildegard of Bingen found on pages 1, 37, 87, 94, 112, 113, 141, and 162 of this book are from Gabriele Uhlein's *Meditations with Hildegard of Bingen: A Centering Book* (©1983) and are used with permission of Inner Traditions/Bear & Company, Rochester, Vermont.

The quotes from Meister Eckhart found on pages 2, 62, 116, 134, and 139 of this book are from Matthew Fox's *Meditations with Meister Eckhart: A Centering Book* (©1983) and are used with permission of Inner Traditions/Bear & Company, Rochester, Vermont.

The quote from Hildegard of Bingen found on page 111 of this book is from Matthew Fox's *Illuminations of Hildegard of Bingen: A Centering Book* (©1985) and is used with permission of Inner Traditions/Bear & Company, Rochester, Vermont.

The quotes found on pages 114 and 137 of this book are from *Herbs and the Earth* by Henry Beston and are reprinted by permission of David R. Godine, Publisher, Boston, Massachusetts. Copyright ©1935 by Henry Beston.

The incense-making activity found on page 151 of this book is adapted from *Gifts & Crafts from the Garden* by Maggie Oster, published by Rodale Press (©1988) and is used with permission of the publisher.

The activities called Egyptian-Style Thanksgiving Garland and Egyptian Floral Bouquet found on pages 84 and 96 of this book are adapted from *An Ancient Egyptian Herbal* by Lise Manniche, published by the University of Texas Press (©1989), and are used with permission of the publisher.

Portions of the information about Abenaki medicine, healing, and herbal traditions in this book are adapted from passages in *A Time Before New Hampshire: The Story of a Land and Native Peoples*. Copyright ©2003 by Michael J. Caduto. Reprinted by permission of the University Press of New England, Hanover, New Hampshire.

The recipes called Easter Carnival (Rustic) Pie, Pepper Biscuits & Pepper Sticks and Milk Biscuits found on pages 64–66, and 108 of this book are adapted from *Gramma's Best Italian Desserts*. Copyright ©1999 by Michael J. Caduto, Esther M. Caduto and Linda A. Caduto. Used with permission from the editors and Green Heart Books.

Children's Spirituality

Does God Forgive Me?
by August Gold; Full-color photos by Diane Hardy Waller
Gently shows how God forgives all that we do if we are truly sorry.
10 x 8½, 32 pp, Quality PB, Full-color photos, 978-1-59473-142-6 **$8.99** *For ages 3–6*

How Does God Listen? *by Kay Lindahl; Full-color photos by Cynthia Maloney*
How do we know when God is listening to us? Children will find the answers to these questions as they engage their senses while the story unfolds, learning how God listens in the wind, waves, clouds, hot chocolate, perfume, our tears and our laughter.
10 x 8½, 32 pp, Quality PB, Full-color photos, 978-1-59473-084-9 **$8.99** *For ages 3–6*

In God's Hands
by Lawrence Kushner and Gary Schmidt; Full-color illus. by Matthew J. Baeck
9 x 12, 32 pp, Full-color illus., HC, 978-1-58023-224-1 **$16.99**
For ages 5 & up (a Jewish Lights book)

In God's Name *by Sandy Eisenberg Sasso; Full-color illus. by Phoebe Stone*
Like an ancient myth in its poetic text and vibrant illustrations, this award-winning modern fable about the search for God's name celebrates the diversity and, at the same time, the unity of all the people of the world.
9 x 12, 32 pp, HC, Full-color illus., 978-1-879045-26-2 **$16.99**
For ages 4 & up (a Jewish Lights book)

Also available in Spanish: **El nombre de Dios**
9 x 12, 32 pp, HC, Full-color illus., 978-1-893361-63-8 **$16.95**

In Our Image: God's First Creatures
by Nancy Sohn Swartz; Full-color illus. by Melanie Hall
A playful new twist on the Genesis story—from the perspective of the animals. Celebrates the interconnectedness of nature and the harmony of all living things.
9 x 12, 32 pp, HC, Full-color illus., 978-1-879045-99-6 **$16.95**
For ages 4 & up (a Jewish Lights book)

Noah's Wife: The Story of Naamah
by Sandy Eisenberg Sasso; Full-color illus. by Bethanne Andersen
This new story, based on an ancient text, opens readers' religious imaginations to new ideas about the well-known story of the Flood. When God tells Noah to bring the animals of the world onto the ark, God also calls on Naamah, Noah's wife, to save each plant on Earth.
9 x 12, 32 pp, HC, Full-color illus., 978-1-58023-134-3 **$16.95**
For ages 4 & up (a Jewish Lights book)

Also available: **Naamah:** Noah's Wife (A Board Book)
by Sandy Eisenberg Sasso; Full-color illus. by Bethanne Andersen
5 x 5, 24 pp, Board Book, Full-color illus., 978-1-893361-56-0 **$7.99** *For ages 0–4*

Or phone, fax, mail or e-mail to: SKYLIGHT PATHS Publishing
Sunset Farm Offices, Route 4 • P.O. Box 237 • Woodstock, Vermont 05091
Tel: (802) 457-4000 • Fax: (802) 457-4004 • www.skylightpaths.com
Credit card orders: (800) 962-4544 (8:30AM–5:30PM ET Monday–Friday)
Generous discounts on quantity orders. SATISFACTION GUARANTEED. Prices subject to change.

Children's Spiritual Biography

Ten Amazing People
And How They Changed the World
by Maura D. Shaw; Foreword by Dr. Robert Coles
Full-color illus. by Stephen Marchesi

For ages 7 & up

Black Elk • Dorothy Day • Malcolm X • Mahatma Gandhi • Martin Luther King, Jr. • Mother Teresa • Janusz Korczak • Desmond Tutu • Thich Nhat Hanh • Albert Schweitzer

This vivid, inspirational and authoritative book will open new possibilities for children by telling the stories of how ten of the past century's greatest leaders changed the world in important ways.

8½ x 11, 48 pp, HC, Full-color illus., 978-1-893361-47-8 **$17.95**
For ages 7 & up

Spiritual Biographies for Young People—For ages 7 and up

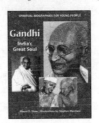

Black Elk: Native American Man of Spirit
by Maura D. Shaw; Full-color illus. by Stephen Marchesi
Through historically accurate illustrations and photos, inspiring age-appropriate activities and Black Elk's own words, this colorful biography introduces children to a remarkable person who ensured that the traditions and beliefs of his people would not be forgotten.
6¾ x 8¾, 32 pp, HC, Full-color and b/w illus., 978-1-59473-043-6 **$12.99**

Dorothy Day: A Catholic Life of Action
by Maura D. Shaw; Full-color illus. by Stephen Marchesi
Introduces children to one of the most inspiring women of the twentieth century, a down-to-earth spiritual leader who saw the presence of God in every person she met. Includes practical activities, a timeline and a list of important words to know.
6¾ x 8¾, 32 pp, HC, Full-color illus., 978-1-59473-011-5 **$12.99**

Gandhi: India's Great Soul
by Maura D. Shaw; Full-color illus. by Stephen Marchesi
There are a number of biographies of Gandhi written for young readers, but this is the only one that balances a simple text with illustrations, photographs, and activities that encourage children and adults to talk about how to make changes happen without violence. Introduces children to important concepts of freedom, equality and justice among people of all backgrounds and religions.
6¾ x 8¾, 32 pp, HC, Full-color illus., 978-1-893361-91-1 **$12.95**

Thich Nhat Hanh: Buddhism in Action
by Maura D. Shaw; Full-color illus. by Stephen Marchesi
Warm illustrations, photos, age-appropriate activities and Thich Nhat Hanh's own poems introduce a great man to children in a way they can understand and enjoy. Includes a list of important Buddhist words to know.
6¾ x 8¾, 32 pp, HC, Full-color illus., 978-1-893361-87-4 **$12.95**

Sacred Texts—SkyLight Illuminations Series

Offers today's spiritual seeker an accessible entry into the great classic texts of the world's spiritual traditions. Each classic is presented in an accessible translation, with facing pages of guided commentary from experts, giving you the keys you need to understand the history, context and meaning of the text. This series enables you, whatever your background, to experience and understand classic spiritual texts directly, and to make them a part of your life.

CHRISTIANITY

The End of Days: Essential Selections from Apocalyptic Texts—
Annotated & Explained *Annotation by Robert G. Clouse*
Helps you understand the complex Christian visions of the end of the world.
5½ x 8½, 224 pp, Quality PB, 978-1-59473-170-9 **$16.99**

The Hidden Gospel of Matthew: Annotated & Explained
Translation & Annotation by Ron Miller
Takes you deep into the text cherished around the world to discover the words and events that have the strongest connection to the historical Jesus.
5½ x 8½, 272 pp, Quality PB, 978-1-59473-038-2 **$16.99**

The Lost Sayings of Jesus: Teachings from Ancient Christian, Jewish,
Gnostic and Islamic Sources—Annotated & Explained
Translation & Annotation by Andrew Phillip Smith; Foreword by Stephan A. Hoeller
This collection of more than three hundred sayings depicts Jesus as a Wisdom teacher who speaks to people of all faiths as a mystic and spiritual master.
5½ x 8½, 240 pp, Quality PB, 978-1-59473-172-3 **$16.99**

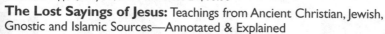

Philokalia: The Eastern Christian Spiritual Texts—Selections Annotated &
Explained *Annotation by Allyne Smith; Translation by G. E. H. Palmer, Phillip Sherrard and Bishop Kallistos Ware*
The first approachable introduction to the wisdom of the Philokalia, which is the classic text of Eastern Christian spirituality.
5½ x 8½, 240 pp, Quality PB, 978-1-59473-103-7 **$16.99**

Spiritual Writings on Mary: Annotated & Explained
Annotation by Mary Ford-Grabowsky; Foreword by Andrew Harvey
Examines the role of Mary, the mother of Jesus, as a source of inspiration in history and in life today. 5½ x 8½, 288 pp, Quality PB, 978-1-59473-001-6 **$16.99**

The Way of a Pilgrim: Annotated & Explained
Translation & Annotation by Gleb Pokrovsky; Foreword by Andrew Harvey
This classic of Russian spirituality is the delightful account of one man who sets out to learn the prayer of the heart, also known as the "Jesus prayer."
5½ x 8½, 160 pp, Illus., Quality PB, 978-1-893361-31-7 **$14.95**

MORMONISM

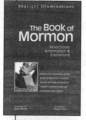

The Book of Mormon: Selections Annotated & Explained
Annotation by Jana Riess; Foreword by Phyllis Tickle
Explores the sacred epic that is cherished by more than twelve million members of the LDS church as the keystone of their faith.
5½ x 8½ , 272 pp, Quality PB, 978-1-59473-076-4 **$16.99**

NATIVE AMERICAN

Native American Stories of the Sacred: Annotated & Explained
Retold & Annotated by Evan T. Pritchard
Intended for more than entertainment, these teaching tales contain elegantly simple illustrations of time-honored truths.
5½ x 8½, 272 pp, Quality PB, 978-1-59473-112-9 **$16.99**

Sacred Texts—cont.

GNOSTICISM

The Gospel of Philip: Annotated & Explained
Translation & Annotation by Andrew Phillip Smith; Foreword by Stevan Davies
Reveals otherwise unrecorded sayings of Jesus and fragments of Gnostic mythology.
5½ x 8½, 160 pp, Quality PB, 978-1-59473-111-2 **$16.99**

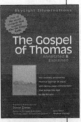

The Gospel of Thomas: Annotated & Explained
Translation & Annotation by Stevan Davies Sheds new light on the origins of Christianity and portrays Jesus as a wisdom-loving sage. 5½ x 8½, 192 pp, Quality PB, 978-1-893361-45-4 **$16.99**

The Secret Book of John: The Gnostic Gospel—Annotated & Explained
Translation & Annotation by Stevan Davies The most significant and influential text of the ancient Gnostic religion. 5½ x 8½, 208 pp, Quality PB, 978-1-59473-082-5 **$16.99**

JUDAISM

The Divine Feminine in Biblical Wisdom Literature
Selections Annotated & Explained
Translation & Annotation by Rabbi Rami Shapiro; Foreword by Rev. Cynthia Bourgeault, PhD
Uses the Hebrew books of Psalms, Proverbs, Song of Songs, Ecclesiastes and Job, Wisdom literature and the Wisdom of Solomon to clarify who Wisdom is.
5½ x 8½, 240 pp, Quality PB, 978-1-59473-109-9 **$16.99**

Ethics of the Sages: *Pirke Avot*—Annotated & Explained
Translation & Annotation by Rabbi Rami Shapiro Clarifies the ethical teachings of the early Rabbis. 5½ x 8½, 192 pp, Quality PB, 978-1-59473-207-2 **$16.99**

Hasidic Tales: Annotated & Explained
Translation & Annotation by Rabbi Rami Shapiro
Introduces the legendary tales of the impassioned Hasidic rabbis, presenting them as stories rather than as parables. 5½ x 8½, 240 pp, Quality PB, 978-1-893361-86-7 **$16.95**

The Hebrew Prophets: Selections Annotated & Explained
Translation & Annotation by Rabbi Rami Shapiro; Foreword by Zalman M. Schachter-Shalomi
Focuses on the central themes covered by all the Hebrew prophets.
5½ x 8½, 224 pp, Quality PB, 978-1-59473-037-5 **$16.99**

Zohar: Annotated & Explained *Translation & Annotation by Daniel C. Matt*
The best-selling author of *The Essential Kabbalah* brings together in one place the most important teachings of the Zohar, the canonical text of Jewish mystical tradition.
5½ x 8½, 176 pp, Quality PB, 978-1-893361-51-5 **$15.99**

EASTERN RELIGIONS

Bhagavad Gita: Annotated & Explained *Translation by Shri Purohit Swami*
Annotation by Kendra Crossen Burroughs Explains references and philosophical terms, shares the interpretations of famous spiritual leaders and scholars, and more.
5½ x 8½, 192 pp, Quality PB, 978-1-893361-28-7 **$16.95**

Dhammapada: Annotated & Explained *Translation by Max Müller and revised by Jack Maguire; Annotation by Jack Maguire* Contains all of Buddhism's key teachings.
5½ x 8½, 160 pp, b/w photos, Quality PB, 978-1-893361-42-3 **$14.95**

Rumi and Islam: Selections from His Stories, Poems, and Discourses—
Annotated & Explained *Translation & Annotation by Ibrahim Gamard*
Focuses on Rumi's place within the Sufi tradition of Islam, providing insight into the mystical side of the religion. 5½ x 8½, 240 pp, Quality PB, 978-1-59473-002-3 **$15.99**

Selections from the Gospel of Sri Ramakrishna: Annotated & Explained
Translation by Swami Nikhilananda; Annotation by Kendra Crossen Burroughs
Introduces the fascinating world of the Indian mystic and the universal appeal of his message. 5½ x 8½, 240 pp, b/w photos, Quality PB, 978-1-893361-46-1 **$16.95**

Tao Te Ching: Annotated & Explained *Translation & Annotation by Derek Lin*
Foreword by Lama Surya Das Introduces an Eastern classic in an accessible, poetic and completely original way. 5½ x 8½, 192 pp, Quality PB, 978-1-59473-204-1 **$16.99**

Spiritual Poetry—The Mystic Poets

Experience these mystic poets as you never have before. Each beautiful, compact book includes: a brief introduction to the poet's time and place; a summary of the major themes of the poet's mysticism and religious tradition; essential selections from the poet's most important works; and an appreciative preface by a contemporary spiritual writer.

Hafiz: The Mystic Poets
Preface by Ibrahim Gamard

Hafiz is known throughout the world as Persia's greatest poet, with sales of his poems in Iran today only surpassed by those of the Qur'an itself. His probing and joyful verse speaks to people from all backgrounds who long to taste and feel divine love and experience harmony with all living things.

5 x 7¼, 144 pp, HC, 978-1-59473-009-2 **$16.99**

Hopkins: The Mystic Poets
Preface by Rev. Thomas Ryan, CSP

Gerard Manley Hopkins, Christian mystical poet, is beloved for his use of fresh language and startling metaphors to describe the world around him. Although his verse is lovely, beneath the surface lies a searching soul, wrestling with and yearning for God.

5 x 7¼, 112 pp, HC, 978-1-59473-010-8 **$16.99**

Tagore: The Mystic Poets
Preface by Swami Adiswarananda

Rabindranath Tagore is often considered the "Shakespeare" of modern India. A great mystic, Tagore was the teacher of W. B. Yeats and Robert Frost, the close friend of Albert Einstein and Mahatma Gandhi, and the winner of the Nobel Prize for Literature. This beautiful sampling of Tagore's two most important works, *The Gardener* and *Gitanjali,* offers a glimpse into his spiritual vision that has inspired people around the world.

5 x 7¼, 144 pp, HC, 978-1-59473-008-5 **$16.99**

Whitman: The Mystic Poets
Preface by Gary David Comstock

Walt Whitman was the most innovative and influential poet of the nineteenth century. This beautiful sampling of Whitman's most important poetry from *Leaves of Grass,* and selections from his prose writings, offers a glimpse into the spiritual side of his most radical themes—love for country, love for others, and love of Self.

5 x 7¼, 192 pp, HC, 978-1-59473-041-2 **$16.99**

Meditation / Prayer

Prayers to an Evolutionary God
by William Cleary; Afterword by Diarmuid O'Murchu
How is it possible to pray when God is dislocated from heaven, dispersed all around us, and more of a creative force than an all-knowing father? Inspired by the spiritual and scientific teachings of Diarmuid O'Murchu and Teilhard de Chardin, Cleary reveals that religion and science can be combined to create an expanding view of the universe—an evolutionary faith.
6 x 9, 208 pp, HC, 978-1-59473-006-1 **$21.99**

Psalms: A Spiritual Commentary
by M. Basil Pennington, OCSO; Illustrations by Phillip Ratner
Showing how the Psalms give profound and candid expression to both our highest aspirations and our deepest pain, the late, highly respected Cistercian Abbot M. Basil Pennington shares his reflections on some of the most beloved passages from the Bible's most widely read book.
6 x 9, 176 pp, HC, 24 full-page b/w illus., 978-1-59473-141-9 **$19.99**

The Song of Songs: A Spiritual Commentary
by M. Basil Pennington, OCSO; Illustrations by Phillip Ratner
Join the late M. Basil Pennington as he ruminates on the Bible's most challenging mystical text. Follow a path into the Songs that weaves through his inspired words and the evocative drawings of Jewish artist Phillip Ratner—a path that reveals your own humanity and leads to the deepest delight of your soul.
6 x 9, 160 pp, HC, 14 b/w illus., 978-1-59473-004-7 **$19.99**

Women of Color Pray: Voices of Strength, Faith, Healing, Hope and Courage *Edited and with Introductions by Christal M. Jackson*
Through these prayers, poetry, lyrics, meditations and affirmations, you will share in the strong and undeniable connection women of color share with God. It will challenge you to explore new ways of prayerful expression.
5 x 7¼, 208 pp, Quality PB, 978-1-59473-077-1 **$15.99**

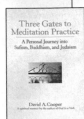

The Art of Public Prayer: Not for Clergy Only
by Lawrence A. Hoffman
An ecumenical resource for all people looking to change hardened worship patterns.
6 x 9, 288 pp, Quality PB, 978-1-893361-06-5 **$18.99**

Finding Grace at the Center, 3rd Ed.: The Beginning of Centering Prayer
by M. Basil Pennington, OCSO, Thomas Keating, OCSO, and Thomas E. Clarke, SJ
Foreword by Rev. Cynthia Bourgeault, PhD
5 x 7¼, 128 pp, Quality PB, 978-1-59473-182-2 **$12.99**

A Heart of Stillness: A Complete Guide to Learning the Art of Meditation
by David A. Cooper 5½ x 8½, 272 pp, Quality PB, 978-1-893361-03-4 **$16.95**

Meditation without Gurus: A Guide to the Heart of Practice
by Clark Strand 5½ x 8½, 192 pp, Quality PB, 978-1-893361-93-5 **$16.95**

Praying with Our Hands: 21 Practices of Embodied Prayer from the World's
Spiritual Traditions *by Jon M. Sweeney; Photographs by Jennifer J. Wilson; Foreword by Mother Tessa Bielecki; Afterword by Taitetsu Unno, PhD*
8 x 8, 96 pp, 22 duotone photos, Quality PB, 978-1-893361-16-4 **$16.95**

Silence, Simplicity & Solitude: A Complete Guide to Spiritual Retreat at Home
by David A. Cooper 5½ x 8½, 336 pp, Quality PB, 978-1-893361-04-1 **$16.95**

Three Gates to Meditation Practice: A Personal Journey into Sufism, Buddhism, and Judaism *by David A. Cooper* 5½ x 8½, 240 pp, Quality PB, 978-1-893361-22-5 **$16.95**

Women Pray: Voices through the Ages, from Many Faiths, Cultures and Traditions
Edited and with Introductions by Monica Furlong
5 x 7¼, 256 pp, Quality PB, 978-1-59473-071-9 **$15.99**
Deluxe HC with ribbon marker, 978-1-893361-25-6 **$19.95**

Spirituality & Crafts

The Knitting Way: A Guide to Spiritual Self-Discovery
by Linda Skolnik and Janice MacDaniels
7 x 9, 240 pp, Quality PB, b/w photographs, 978-1-59473-079-5 **$16.99**

The Quilting Path: A Guide to Spiritual Discovery through Fabric, Thread and Kabbalah
by Louise Silk
7 x 9, 192 pp, Quality PB, b/w photographs and illustrations, 978-1-59473-206-5 **$16.99**

The Scrapbooking Journey: A Hands-On Guide to Spiritual Discovery
by Cory Richardson-Lauve; Foreword by Stacy Julian
7 x 9, 176 pp, Quality PB, 8-page full-color insert, plus b/w photographs
978-1-59473-216-4 **$18.99**

Spiritual Practice

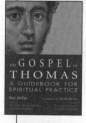

Divining the Body: Reclaim the Holiness of Your Physical Self
by Jan Phillips
A practical and inspiring guidebook for connecting the body and soul in spiritual practice. Leads you into a milieu of reverence, mystery and delight, helping you discover your body as a pathway to the Divine.
8 x 8, 256 pp, Quality PB, 978-1-59473-080-1 **$16.99**

Finding Time for the Timeless: Spirituality in the Workweek
by John McQuiston II
Simple, refreshing stories that provide you with examples of how you can refocus and enrich your daily life using prayer or meditation, ritual and other forms of spiritual practice. 5½ x 6¾, 208 pp, HC, 978-1-59473-035-1 **$17.99**

The Gospel of Thomas: A Guidebook for Spiritual Practice
by Ron Miller; Translations by Stevan Davies
An innovative guide to bring a new spiritual classic into daily life.
6 x 9, 160 pp, Quality PB, 978-1-59473-047-4 **$14.99**

Earth, Water, Fire, and Air: Essential Ways of Connecting to Spirit
by Cait Johnson 6 x 9, 224 pp, HC, 978-1-893361-65-2 **$19.95**

Labyrinths from the Outside In: Walking to Spiritual Insight—A Beginner's Guide
by Donna Schaper and Carole Ann Camp
6 x 9, 208 pp, b/w illus. and photos, Quality PB, 978-1-893361-18-8 **$16.95**

Practicing the Sacred Art of Listening: A Guide to Enrich Your Relationships and Kindle Your Spiritual Life—The Listening Center Workshop
by Kay Lindahl 8 x 8, 176 pp, Quality PB, 978-1-893361-85-0 **$16.95**

Releasing the Creative Spirit: Unleash the Creativity in Your Life
by Dan Wakefield 7 x 10, 256 pp, Quality PB, 978-1-893361-36-2 **$16.95**

The Sacred Art of Bowing: Preparing to Practice
by Andi Young 5½ x 8½, 128 pp, b/w illus., Quality PB, 978-1-893361-82-9 **$14.95**

The Sacred Art of Chant: Preparing to Practice
by Ana Hernández 5½ x 8½, 192 pp, Quality PB, 978-1-59473-036-8 **$15.99**

The Sacred Art of Fasting: Preparing to Practice
by Thomas Ryan, CSP 5½ x 8½, 192 pp, Quality PB, 978-1-59473-078-8 **$15.99**

The Sacred Art of Forgiveness: Forgiving Ourselves and Others through God's Grace
by Marcia Ford 8 x 8, 176 pp, Quality PB, 978-1-59473-175-4 **$16.99**

The Sacred Art of Listening: Forty Reflections for Cultivating a Spiritual Practice
by Kay Lindahl; Illustrations by Amy Schnapper
8 x 8, 160 pp, b/w illus., Quality PB, 978-1-893361-44-7 **$16.99**

The Sacred Art of Lovingkindness: Preparing to Practice
by Rabbi Rami Shapiro; Foreword by Marcia Ford
5½ x 8½, 176 pp, Quality PB, 978-1-59473-151-8 **$16.99**

Sacred Speech: A Practical Guide for Keeping Spirit in Your Speech
by Rev. Donna Schaper 6 x 9, 176 pp, Quality PB, 978-1-59473-068-9 **$15.99**
HC, 978-1-893361-74-4 **$21.95**

Spirituality of the Seasons

Autumn: A Spiritual Biography of the Season
Edited by Gary Schmidt and Susan M. Felch; Illustrations by Mary Azarian
Rejoice in autumn as a time of preparation and reflection. Includes Wendell Berry, David James Duncan, Robert Frost, A. Bartlett Giamatti, E. B. White, P. D. James, Julian of Norwich, Garret Keizer, Tracy Kidder, Anne Lamott, May Sarton.
6 x 9, 320 pp, 5 b/w illus., Quality PB, 978-1-59473-118-1 **$18.99**
HC, 978-1-59473-005-4 **$22.99**

Spring: A Spiritual Biography of the Season
Edited by Gary Schmidt and Susan M. Felch; Illustrations by Mary Azarian
Explore the gentle unfurling of spring and reflect on how nature celebrates rebirth and renewal. Includes Jane Kenyon, Lucy Larcom, Harry Thurston, Nathaniel Hawthorne, Noel Perrin, Annie Dillard, Martha Ballard, Barbara Kingsolver, Dorothy Wordsworth, Donald Hall, David Brill, Lionel Basney, Isak Dinesen, Paul Laurence Dunbar. 6 x 9, 352 pp, 6 b/w illus., HC, 978-1-59473-114-3 **$21.99**

Summer: A Spiritual Biography of the Season
Edited by Gary Schmidt and Susan M. Felch; Illustrations by Barry Moser
"A sumptuous banquet.... These selections lift up an exquisite wholeness found within an everyday sophistication." — ★ *Publishers Weekly* starred review
Includes Anne Lamott, Luci Shaw, Ray Bradbury, Richard Selzer, Thomas Lynch, Walt Whitman, Carl Sandburg, Sherman Alexie, Madeleine L'Engle, Jamaica Kincaid.
6 x 9, 304 pp, 5 b/w illus., Quality PB, 978-1-59473-183-9 **$18.99**
HC, 978-1-59473-083-2 **$21.99**

Winter: A Spiritual Biography of the Season
Edited by Gary Schmidt and Susan M. Felch; Illustrations by Barry Moser
"This outstanding anthology features top-flight nature and spirituality writers on the fierce, inexorable season of winter.... Remarkably lively and warm, despite the icy subject." — ★ *Publishers Weekly* starred review.
Includes Will Campbell, Rachel Carson, Annie Dillard, Donald Hall, Ron Hansen, Jane Kenyon, Jamaica Kincaid, Barry Lopez, Kathleen Norris, John Updike, E. B. White.
6 x 9, 288 pp, 6 b/w illus., Deluxe PB w/flaps, 978-1-893361-92-8 **$18.95**
HC, 978 1 893361-53-9 **$21.95**

Spirituality / Animal Companions

Blessing the Animals: Prayers and Ceremonies to Celebrate God's Creatures, Wild and Tame *Edited by Lynn L. Caruso* 5 x 7¼, 256 pp, HC, 978-1-59473-145-7 **$19.99**

What Animals Can Teach Us about Spirituality: Inspiring Lessons from Wild and Tame Creatures *by Diana L. Guerrero* 6 x 9, 176 pp, Quality PB, 978-1-893361-84-3 **$16.95**

Spirituality

Awakening the Spirit, Inspiring the Soul
30 Stories of Interspiritual Discovery in the Community of Faiths
Edited by Brother Wayne Teasdale and Martha Howard, MD; Foreword by Joan Borysenko, PhD
Thirty original spiritual mini-autobiographies showcase the varied ways that people come to faith—and what that means—in today's multi-religious world.
6 x 9, 224 pp, HC, 978-1-59473-039-9 **$21.99**

The Alphabet of Paradise: An A–Z of Spirituality for Everyday Life
by Howard Cooper 5 x 7¾, 224 pp, Quality PB, 978-1-893361-80-5 **$16.95**

Creating a Spiritual Retirement: A Guide to the Unseen Possibilities in Our Lives
by Molly Srode 6 x 9, 208 pp, b/w photos, Quality PB, 978-1-59473-050-4 **$14.99**
HC, 978-1-893361-75-1 **$19.95**

Finding Hope: Cultivating God's Gift of a Hopeful Spirit
by Marcia Ford 8 x 8, 200 pp, Quality PB, 978-1-59473-211-9 **$16.99**

The Geography of Faith: Underground Conversations on Religious, Political and Social Change *by Daniel Berrigan and Robert Coles* 6 x 9, 224 pp, Quality PB, 978-1-893361-40-9 **$16.95**

God Within: Our Spiritual Future—As Told by Today's New Adults *Edited by Jon M. Sweeney and the Editors at SkyLight Paths* 6 x 9, 176 pp, Quality PB, 978-1-893361-15-7 **$14.95**

About SKYLIGHT PATHS Publishing

SkyLight Paths Publishing is creating a place where people of different spiritual traditions come together for challenge and inspiration, a place where we can help each other understand the mystery that lies at the heart of our existence.

Through spirituality, our religious beliefs are increasingly becoming a part of our lives—rather than *apart* from our lives. While many of us may be more interested than ever in spiritual growth, we may be less firmly planted in traditional religion. Yet, we do want to deepen our relationship to the sacred, to learn from our own as well as from other faith traditions, and to practice in new ways.

SkyLight Paths sees both believers and seekers as a community that increasingly transcends traditional boundaries of religion and denomination—people wanting to learn from each other, *walking together, finding the way*.

For your information and convenience, at the back of this book we have provided a list of other SkyLight Paths books you might find interesting and useful. They cover the following subjects:

Buddhism / Zen	Gnosticism	Mysticism
Catholicism	Hinduism /	Poetry
Children's Books	Vedanta	Prayer
Christianity	Inspiration	Religious Etiquette
Comparative	Islam / Sufism	Retirement
Religion	Judaism / Kabbalah /	Spiritual Biography
Current Events	Enneagram	Spiritual Direction
Earth-Based	Meditation	Spirituality
Spirituality	Midrash Fiction	Women's Interest
Global Spiritual	Monasticism	Worship
Perspectives		